Stepping Stones to Women's Liberty

Feminist ideas in the women's suffrage
movement 1900–1918

Les Garner

Rutherford · Madison · Teaneck
Fairleigh Dickinson University Press

For Ann

© Les Garner 1984
First American edition 1984.

Associated University Presses
440 Forsgate Drive
Cranbury, New Jersey 08512

Library of Congress Cataloging in Publication Data

Garner, Les.
  Stepping stones to women's liberty.

  Bibliography: p.
  Includes index.
    1. Women–Suffrage—Great Britain—History—20th
century.   2. Feminism—Great Britain—History–20th
century.   I. Title.
JN979.G37   1984   324.6 '23 '0941   83-25360
ISBN 0-8386-3223-8

Printed in Great Britain

Contents

List of Illustrations

Acknowledgements: **3**, **16** courtesy of the Museum of London; **10**
courtesy of Syndication International Library; **13** courtesy of Mrs Bate;
all others by kind permission of the British Library.

Acknowledgements

For help, encouragement and support I would like to thank: Ann Hughes who originally interested me in feminism – without Ann's help this book or the thesis it is based on would have never been written; Sue Sharpe and Sheila Rowbotham, who encouraged my research in the early days (I owe a general debt to Sheila's voluminous outpourings, too); Mildred Surrey and David Doughan, past librarian and present worker at the Fawcett Library; Wilhelmina Schroeder of the Institute of Social History, Amsterdam (Sylvia Pankhurst papers); Mrs Bate of Prestatyn (Marsden papers); Anna Davin and Sally Alexander for their criticisms of my work on *The Freewoman*; David Morgan, my supervisor at Liverpool University, for his unceasing advice and positive criticism of my thesis; David Hill and Caroline Lane at Heinemann; Eve Gordon, who typed with remarkable skill and efficiency; Nicola Mezzotti, who finished this manuscript when Eve was unable to continue because of illness; Esther Eisenthal for her meticulous editing of the manuscript; my friends at Canonbury Road, Campbell Buildings and Southwark College where Sandy Llewellyn gave me much pertinent advice and help with the index; and finally to Pete, Marion, Polly and especially Pauline who somehow managed to put up with me while this book was being written. None of the above are responsible for what follows but I hope they, and Charlotte, too, will enjoy it.

Oh Holloway, grim Holloway,
With grey forbidding towers!
Stern are thy walls, but sterner still
Is Woman's free, unconquered will,
And though today and yesterday
Brought long and lonely hours,
Those hours spent in captivity
Are stepping stones to liberty.

Women in Prison by Kathleen Emerson
(N.A. John ed., *Holloway Jingles*,
Women's Social and Political Union, 1912)

. . . the present demand, in the minds of the majority of its advocates, is a mere stepping stone to something far more extensive and revolutionary.

(*The Franchise for Women of Property*,
Women's National Anti-Suffrage League, 1908)

If there is, lying dormant, one spark of latent desire for freedom, for growth, you have some ground to work on, some hope of results. And one of the best means, I rather think, of appealing to this dormant quality is to rouse a sense of resentment against obvious inequality, as in the voteless condition of women compared with men. It may be this, merely, at first. But first steps must be taken.

Ada Nield Chew
(*The Freewoman* April 18, 1912)

Introduction

This book examines the feminism of an early twentieth-century movement that involved thousands of women – the struggle for the vote. It is
not a narrative account of how the vote was won, nor is it yet another
record of the tactics of the suffragettes. Instead, it is an attempt to
discover some of the main ideas developed within the major suffragist
organisations: the National Union of Women's Suffrage Societies
(NUWSS), the Women's Freedom League (WFL) and the Pankhursts'
Women's Social and Political Union (WSPU). How did they identify
the oppression of women and what solutions did they propose?

The traditional approach to the women's suffrage movement has not
asked this and is in other ways flawed. It has usually been centred on the
Pankhursts and has concentrated on their militant tactics (D. Mitchell
1966, 1967; Raeburn 1973). It has not only assumed that militant
tactics reflected a militant ideology but it has ignored the importance of
the NUWSS and the WFL. This book intends to counter these distor-
tions. The contribution of the 'non-militants' to the suffrage campaign
was arguably greater than that of the WSPU, and their dull and boring
image is inaccurate. Furthermore, the limited literature on the
NUWSS (Strachey 1928; Kamm 1966) has tended to concentrate on the
tactics of the campaign, and not on the ideas of the women's suffrage
movement; and another shortcoming is that the WFL has only cropped
up as part of the history of the WSPU, although there has been a recent
biography of its president, Charlotte Despard (Linklater 1980). Few
have attempted a wider assessment of suffragism (Rover 1970; Harrison 1978) and none have matched the excellent *One Hand Tied Behind
Us* (Liddington and Norris 1978) which looks at radical suffragists in
the industrial North.

In short, the feminism of the women's suffrage movement in England has either been ill-defined or, as with the WSPU, misrepresented.
Yet determining 'suffragist feminism' is beset with many problems in
terms of material, scope and approach. It would, for example, be
fruitless to attempt to formulate a single suffragist manifesto of feminist
ideas and prescriptions. There were different emphases within each of
the main organisations, and 'suffragist feminism' was in fact both fluid
and eclectic. It is more useful to regard the ideas within the movement
as part of a continuing debate, although some fixed positions and
boundaries can be identified. Another problem is that, by reviewing the

ideas expressed within national suffragist papers and literature, a centralised picture is bound to emerge. This is particularly so with the NUWSS which had nearly 500 affiliated societies by 1914; it is hoped that more local studies will follow Liddington and Norris. There is also the problem of evaluation. Particular care must be taken not to 'judge' suffragist feminism by modern standards nor to ignore the suffragists' own social and political environment. This is why a brief survey of how that environment affected women, along with the later chapters on *The Freewoman* and Sylvia Pankhurst, are vital to an assessment of suffragism.

What follows, then, aims to be a contribution towards a fuller understanding of the feminism of the women's suffrage movement – one volume alone could not hope to cover every aspect of the movement. It is an enquiry that reflects contemporary concerns and issues: How did this women's movement define the oppression of women, and how did it assess the roles of the sexes and the sexual division of labour? What perspectives were adopted on sexuality and reproduction? How did suffragists organise and how did they view the value of legislative reform? How did the movement relate to working class women? These questions are guided by an attitude that recognises the oppression of women as a sex but which also emphasises the importance of class. It is true that women were oppressed before the development of capitalism, and their oppression as a sex has to be recognised. But it is difficult to conceive of their liberation within a society that is based on economic inequality and which so heavily defines and exploits their 'natural' roles. Finally, this attitude is also based on the notion that, as one woman put it over 70 years ago, 'The Freewoman wants no ready sphere . . . The Freewoman wants the whole round earth to choose from' (Caroline Boord, *The Freewoman* December 14, 1911:70).

London 1983

1 Feminism and the 1900s: some influences on suffragism

Ideas do not come from heaven but from reactions to particular social and political environments. They are shaped, too, by tradition and by the history and experience of past struggles. Thus a brief understanding of the ideological heritage of suffragism and the political context within which it operated is necessary to a discussion of its ideas. However, what follows is not, and does not pretend to be, a comprehensive account either of the development of feminism or of early twentieth-century politics, but is an analysis of their possible influence on suffragist thought.

Modern feminism, though hidden from history for so long, can be traced back to the seventeenth century and the advent of capitalism. An unequal power relationship between the sexes existed before the dawn of the new economic system but capitalism had a significant effect on the position of women. In particular, as the function of the family, as a self-sufficient economic unit, declined, capitalism devalued women's role in production. The growth of production and waged labour outside the home changed the interdependent relationship between husband and wife and 'led to the identification of family life with privacy, home consumption, domesticity – and with women' (R. Hamilton 1978:18). Home was no longer central to production and became, ideally, a domestic haven of peace and tranquillity. Women's place was in the home: the concept of separate spheres had arrived.

This was neither a simple nor a uniform process, and it affected women in different ways. Working class women became burdened both by the new domestic ideology and by work outside the home. Bourgeois women, on the other hand, although materially satisfied, were encouraged to adopt the role of the weak and helpless creature, lost without a man and suited to no work other than pleasing him and raising his children. As Milton wrote, 'He for God only and she for God in him'.

Placed on a pedestal but bored by their idleness and dissatisfied by their new role, some middle class women began to articulate their grievances. 'Sophia', for example, wrote in 1739, in *Woman not Inferior to Man*, that men felt women were 'fit only to breed and nurse children . . . to mind household affairs and to obey, serve and please our masters, that is, themselves, forsooth'. Mary Wollstonecraft, in her *Vindication of the Rights of Women* (1792), similarly attacked 'the weak elegancy of mind, exquisite sensibility and sweet docility of manners, supposed to be the sexual characteristics of the weaker vessel'. She wanted to show that 'elegance is inferior to virtue, that the first object of laudable ambition is to obtain a character as human being, regardless of the distinction of sex' (1792:7).

In retrospect, women such as these were laying their claim to an equality promised by the new bourgeois ideology of liberalism. They could see no logical reason why women should not share the same rights as men since both sexes were part of a common humanity. At the same time, they shared the limits of that ideology too, particularly in regard to economic equality (Mitchell and Oakley 1976:379–99). Furthermore, Wollstonecraft appeared to believe that men ultimately would be converted through the sheer logic of her case. Both arguments became a part of the suffragist heritage.

English feminism from the beginning, however, had many different components. The exploitation of working class women and their involvement in early trade union, socialist and radical groups ultimately led to a feminism which argued that emancipation could only be achieved through drastic political and economic change. One of the earliest examples of this was William Thompson's *Appeal of One Half of the Human Race, Women, Against the Pretensions of the Other Half, Men, to Retain Them in Political and Thence Civil and Domestic Slavery* (1825). Written in response to an article by James Mill which claimed that women's interests were adequately represented by men, Thompson stated (in the words of Sylvia Pankhurst's son), 'that the championship of the emancipation of women was interrelated to opposition to private property, the state and organised religion' (R.K.P. Pankhurst 1954). Written with the help of his feminist companion, Anna Wheeler, the *Appeal* was a passionate attack on the position of women and a cry for their freedom: married women, for example, were little more than 'involuntary breeding machines and household slaves', each one living in a home that was her 'eternal prison house' (*ibid.*: 83–4). Although the *Appeal* itself could only have had a limited circulation, the linking of emancipation with wider social and economic factors in early radical and socialist thinking established a division within English feminism: 'from this point on the conflict was explicit between the two feminisms, one seeking acceptance in the bourgeois world, the other seeking another world altogether' (Rowbotham 1974:50).

But, although these two major currents within English feminism had been established by the nineteenth century (Saywell 1936), neither remained static. In particular, there was a growing emphasis within liberal feminism on what was regarded as the biologically determined roles and characteristics of the sexes. Society was unbalanced because women's domestic and maternal virtues were neglected. As Anne

Knight, of the Sheffield Association for the Female Franchise, stated in 1851, no state could be well governed until 'both sexes . . . are fairly represented, and have an influence . . . in the enactment and administration of our laws . . . The wise, virtuous, gentle mothers of a state or nation might contribute as much to the good order, the peace, the thrift of the body politic, as they severally do to the well being of their families' (Blackburn 1902:19).

Both the classic argument within liberal feminism (that women should share the same rights as men because of their common humanity), and the notion that they did after all have particular roles and characteristics, were evident in John Stuart Mill's famous *On the Subjection of Women* (1869). Mill believed that equality could come through reform and he had unsuccessfully proposed a women's suffrage amendment to the Second Reform Bill in 1866. In *On the Subjection of Women*, Mill argued that the principles of equality and freedom of choice should apply to both sexes and he was critical of the socialisation of women. 'What is now called the nature of women is an eminently artificial thing – the result of forced oppression in some directions, unnatural stimulations in others' (1869:38). But Mill implicitly seemed to accept that there were, after all, 'natural' roles for men and women: 'the common arrangement by which the man earns the income and the wife superintends the domestic expenditure, seems to me in general the most suitable division of labour between the two' (*ibid.*: 87). He also felt that, in any case, only a few women would take advantage of equal opportunities as a result of 'the preference always likely to be felt by the majority of women for the one vocation in which there is nobody to compete with them' [motherhood and childcare] (*ibid.*:93).

How far are these early arguments, with their contradictions, visible also within the feminism of the suffragists? Certainly, the argument that women's rights should be extended so that their special qualities could be brought to bear on the state, seemed to gather momentum in the latter half of the century. F.P. Cobbe, in her *Duties of Women* (1881), for example, made this very clear. She argued that the natural role of women was in the home and that 'for a woman to fail to make and keep a happy home, is to be a "failure" in a truer sense than to have failed to catch a husband' (1881:114). Cobbe also emphasised women's natural purity and vocation for motherhood and childcare. It was because womanly virtues were lacking in the government of the state that she demanded greater political rights, including the vote for women.

The other component of feminist thought – socialist feminism – was re-awakened by the resurgence of the socialist movement in the latter part of the nineteenth century. Engels' *Origin of the Family* (1884) associated the oppression of women within the family with the growth of private property and capitalism. The writings of both Engels and Marx suggested that emancipation would only come through women's active involvement in the class struggle outside the home: their liberation could only come through the destruction of the economic system of capitalism. Others, for example, the Sheffield radical, Edward Carpenter, also emphasised specific aspects of women's oppression as a sex. Carpenter's *Loves Coming of Age* (1896:43) was particularly critical of the 'choices' open to women – 'the lady, the household drudge, and the prostitute'. Marriage was only maintained by 'the monetary dependence of the woman, the mere sex needs of the man and the fear of public opinion' (*ibid.*:75). On the other hand, other socialists, such as Blatchford and Hyndman, were either wary of discussing the family or sexuality, or thought they were irrelevant to the class struggle (Rowbotham 1977a:65–73).

Socialists were divided, too, on the very issue of the vote, particularly as it obviously involved the whole debate about revolution or reform. It was complicated further by the suffragist demand for the vote on the same terms as men. Socialists were concerned: the property qualifications for the franchise meant that not all men could vote (Blewitt 1972), so that the suffragist demand for a female vote would place propertied women alone on the electoral register. As this would serve to aid their political opponents, socialists could only logically demand adult suffrage. Yet this invoked opposition not only from those opposed to votes for women but from the powerful lobby against universal suffrage as well (Harrison 1978:33). The problem led to many acrimonious debates with the Labour movement and was a particular dilemma for socialist suffragists, torn between class and sex loyalties.

Some socialists and anarchists thought the struggle for the vote was an irrelevancy anyway. Lily Gair Wilkinson, of the Socialist Labour Party, in her *Revolutionary Socialism and the Woman's Movement* (c.1910), attacked women's suffrage as reformist and believed it would only benefit those 'who belong to the privileged or propertied class in society' (c. 1910:9). For 'women of the working class the practical question is the question of the class antagonism' (*ibid.*). Four years later, in her *Women's Freedom*, Wilkinson adopted a more anarchistic position. She claimed that all women were oppressed through having to sell their bodies 'for men's pleasure or . . . for the profit of an employer' (1914:5). Yet women were driven to this 'not because of the domination of some big abstraction called Man, but because of the domination of those human laws by which both men and women are forbidden the free use and enjoyment of the earth they live upon'; and, although she admired the bravery of the suffragettes, 'votes for women' was 'a poor, cracked, treble call', a diversion from a revolutionary struggle against the state and capitalism (*ibid.*: 5, 9).

But by 1900 the women's suffrage movement enjoyed mass support from thousands of supporters whose views ranged across the political spectrum. Besides the major societies discussed in the following chapters, there was a whole range of organisations, from the Conservative and Unionist Women's Suffrage Association to the Actresses Franchise League, that demanded votes for women. From amendments to the 1832 Reform Bill, through Chartism and Mill's attempt to change the Bill of 1866, the struggle for the vote could be seen as part of the nineteenth-century campaign for electoral reform (Blackburn 1902; Strachey 1928). However, the campaign for the vote in the early twentieth century was not simply part of the unfinished business of parliamentary reform and clearly involved other issues specifically relating to women. What were these issues and why did suffragism attract such mass support?

A major reason for the support given to the women's suffrage movement was the imbalance between the ratio of the sexes. A surplus of women over men prevented women from fulfilling their 'natural' careers of marriage and motherhood. In other words, in an age where 'it was not a question of marrying well . . . any husband was better than none', and where the nursery game 'Old Maid' warned children of the dangers of spinsterhood (Adam 1975:13), the opportunity to get married was declining. In 1851 there were 1,042 women to every 1,000 men, rising to 1,068 to every 1,000 men by 1911. Moreover, in the early twentieth century the percentage of unmarried women in the critical age band of 20 to 45 years rose as the marriage rate, further affected by an ailing economy, fell (Glass 1938:252–69). Though a somewhat crude index, this was important in terms of fuelling the attempts to legitimise other roles for women, particularly in the push for wider opportunities. Certainly, contemporary theatre (Ibsen's *Doll's House*, Shaw's *Getting Married* and *Man and Superman*) and literature (Well's *Ann Veronica*, Grant Allen's *The Woman Who Did*) reflected an awareness of the problems surrounding single women and marriage. And it is in the light of the push for new areas of work for women that pioneers such as Louisa Twining and Mary Carpenter (philanthropy), Florence Nightingale, Elizabeth Garrett Anderson and Sophia Jex Blake (medicine) and Davies, Clough and Beale (education) should be seen (Strachey 1928).

Another major factor was the inequality of the legal system and how it affected women. The law surrounding husband and wife was particularly unjust. It was the wife who always suffered in cases of guardianship of children, intestacy, tax, divorce and maintenance. As Helena Swanwick, a leading member of the NUWSS put it in *Some Points of English Law Affecting Working Women As Wives and Workers* (1914), a book written for the Women's Co-operative Guild, 'the existing law and administration of law in England gives to women and children very imperfect protection from bad men . . . Cruelty and neglect are practised with large impunity. The sacred rights of the mother are nil, if she is married. The sacred home is broken up whenever a man dies or deserts' (1914:31). The claim by suffragists that voting women would be able to change the law must have been appealing.

Another possible reason for the support given to suffragism was the sexual oppression of women. This was a complex issue. Contemporary morality, while perhaps allowing men's right to enjoy sex, argued that its only function – certainly for women – was procreative. The ideals were innocence, chastity and purity. Prostitution and the White Slave Traffic were the other side of the coin. It was a hypocritical morality, as Josephine Butler's campaign against the Contagious Diseases Acts implied (Strachey 1928). Butler exposed a set of values based in reality on the economic dependence and the sexual oppression of women. On the other hand, demands for greater sexual freedom were treated with suspicion, especially given the contemporary concern over venereal disease. Not surprisingly, many women preferred the ideal of monogamous marriage to the risks of sexual liberation, and they demanded that men live up to the ideals of chastity and fidelity too (Rover 1970).

The control of reproduction was another vital part of this issue – essential to the separation of sex from procreation and to relieving the burden of unwanted pregnancies. It appears that an increasing number of middle class women was using birth control in the latter half of the nineteenth century (Banks 1964). Although it is more difficult to estimate its use among the working class, the existence of large working class families and the apparent growth of dangerous and illegal abortions (Glass 1938; Fryer 1965), surely reflected a need for birth control. There were numerous methods available including the vaginal sponge, the condom and the cap, and the circulation of literature on contraception was, at least among the middle classes, widespread (Fryer 1965). Yet pioneers such as Besant and Bradlaugh were faced with charges of immorality and indecency when they tried to propagandise contraception among the working classes. 'No poison moral or material, was ever offered to mankind so evil as this philosophy,' cried *The Evening Standard* at the Besant–Bradlaugh trial (Banks 1964).

Finally, the position of working women was crucial to suffragism. The WSPU had originally grown out of Northern working class and Labour movement circles while working women were particularly active there in the NUWSS (Liddington and Norris 1978). But working women (that is, those paid for their work) were not just restricted to the industrial North, and their numbers had grown to $4\frac{1}{2}$ million by 1901, and to 5 million by 1914 (Mitchell and Deane 1962:60). They worked in many industries besides the textile industry, a few professions, domestic service, and the aptly labelled 'sweated trades'. Trade unionism among women continued to grow, although by 1914 they only accounted for 17 per cent of all trade unionists (Drake 1920:239). Most working women were overworked and underpaid: Sidney Webb calculated that the average women's wage in 1906 was 10/10½d compared to 25/9d for men (*ibid.*:44). Conditions and pay in the sweated trades were particularly oppressive and were exposed by numerous women's organisations such as the Women's Industrial Council (WIC). One WIC Report, by Clementina Black, a leading member of the NUWSS, stated the obvious: 'The fact is undeniable that these women are not paid for their work a wage upon which they can actually subsist' (Black 1906:44). Thus the oppression of working class women, and their concern about legislation affecting their employment, provided a major pool of support for suffragism.

But the most obvious reason why women supported the suffrage movement was that, as otherwise qualified citizens, they were not allowed the parliamentary vote purely because of their sex. How could women who were doctors, teachers, workers and mothers, suffragists asked, be unfit to vote? If, as their opponents the 'antis' (anti-suffragists) replied, it was because political power was ultimately based on physical force and a citizen's ability to use it – then why were not all the old, sick and invalid men disqualified? Why not have a machine outside the polling booth to test an elector's strength, suffragists mocked; those who could not hit the bell would be turned away.

In fact the opposition to women's suffrage had political causes, more complex perhaps than might appear at a first glance. Although the obstinate opposition of the Prime Minister, Asquith, was an important factor, this alone does not fully explain why votes for women were so long delayed. If women's suffrage was to come, Labour, Liberal and Tory all wanted a measure that would suit their interests. Moreover, there were internal divisions in each of the parties over the issue and much hostility from those opposed to any extension of the franchise.

Votes for women also floundered because it became involved with the struggle over the House of Lords. Until the power of the Lords was curtailed, a franchise bill satisfactory to the Liberals (that is, a wide measure) had little chance of success, given the inbuilt Tory majority in the Upper House. Besides this problem, Irish Nationalists were wary of any electoral reform since a new parliamentary register could endanger their strength in Parliament. Consequently, they often abstained or voted against women's suffrage bills. With the heavy load of legislation *and* the Prime Minister's personal hostility, the suffragist cause was clearly faced with considerable obstacles. (This is discussed further in chapter 7.) This again shows the limitations of the view of the women's suffrage struggle as a simple battle between the Pankhursts and Asquith (Morgan 1975).

It would be an equally inadequate view to regard votes for women as the only important political issue of the turbulent 1900s. With constitutional crises over the House of Lords and Ireland, and the growth of militant class struggle in industry, it sometimes appeared that the political system was about to collapse. The years from 1906 to 1914 'witnessed a crescendo of rule breaking . . . until the fabric of democracy came into real danger' (Ensor 1936:398). The Mother of Parliaments had become just 'so many square yards in Westminster; so many feet of talkative air . . . so many echoes in an inconvenient chamber where several hundred gentlemen sullenly debated' (Dangerfield 1970:131).

The relative decline of the economy, faced with internal problems and competition from abroad, was a key factor to this instability. It led ultimately to a fall in the value of wages, a rise in unemployment and even sharper divisions of wealth. The surveys of Booth and Rowntree suggested that at the turn of the century a third of the population lived on or below the poverty line. Jack London's *People of The Abyss* (1903) described graphically the life of the poor in Edwardian England. Clearly references to an Edwardian 'Golden Age' were unfounded, for 'wealth, luxury and indolence were restricted to a very small section of society, a well to do stratum poised above an abyss of poverty, misery and discontent' (Kendall 1969:24).

These factors contributed considerably to the growth of militant class struggle. From 1910 onwards there was a series of strikes in vital sections of the economy, including the docks, the mines, railways and shipping: in 1912 alone 38 million working days were lost due to strikes (*ibid*.:27). At the same time, a growing dissatisfaction with the leadership of the Labour movement further fuelled rank and file militancy. All this resulted in increasingly violent clashes between workers and, on the one hand, their employers, and, on the other, the state, and a growing use of police and army in industrial disputes. Liberal England, especially after 1910, witnessed 'soldiers up and down the country, generals directing the traffic on the railways, shootings and explosions' (Dangerfield 1970:242). In such a whirlpool did the suffragist fish swim.

This environment affected women in several ways, some more obvious than others. Growing unemployment led to increasing pressure on women workers, especially married women workers, to return to the domestic sphere. As John Burns, President of the Board of Trade, argued, in a depressingly familiar tone, 'Women's labour, especially married women's labour, must be enormously curtailed' (*The Times* December 10, 1907:12). A more subtle way in which the state of the economy and the fear of competition from abroad affected women was in relation to the growing concern over the health and size of the population. This concern partly fuelled the development of social reform, the quest for natural efficiency and, allied to fears of a falling birth rate, the calls for a fit and healthy race (Davin 1978). Lord Rosebury, a leading advocate of imperialism, demanded that: 'An Empire such as ours requires as its first condition an imperial race – a race vigorous, industrious and intrepid . . . in the rookeries and the slums which still survive, an imperial race cannot be reared' (Semmel 1960:62).

There was therefore extra pressure on women to adopt a maternal role: the 'need to breed an imperial race in Britain if the Empire was to remain British and strong' (*ibid.*:28) led to 'a surge of concern about the bearing of children – the next generation of soldiers and workers' (Davin 1978:12). In short, a cult of motherhood developed aided to some extent by the state and by numerous voluntary organisations such as the Women's League of Service for Motherhood. If a woman's role was 'naturally' in the home, the contemporary pressures further pushed her there. It was a powerful impulse, alongside growing unemployment, towards confirming the sexual division of labour and the belief, expressed by Major General Sir Frederick Maurice in 1903, that 'for the raising of a virile race, either of soldiers or of citizens, it is essential that the attention of the mothers of the land should be mainly devoted to the three K's – Kinder, Kuche, Kirche' [Children, Kitchen and Church] (*ibid.*:16).

Fears about the fitness of the nation and the Empire allied to concern over the growing military might of Germany, also emphasised the male 'virtues' of power and strength. It is hardly surprising that army reform was a current issue or that both the Boy Scouts and the Officer Training Corps were established during this period. Any confusion of 'natural' sex roles, or any movement that appeared to threaten those roles, had to be opposed – by men concerned about their power over women, and by the ruling élite as a whole. As Lord Cromer, the leader of the anti-suffragists, stated in 1910: 'can we hope to compete with such a nation as this [Germany] if we war against nature, and endeavour to invert the natural roles of the sexes? We cannot do so' (*Anti-Suffrage Review* 1910).

Thus the political and social context within which the suffrage movement operated was extremely complex and appeared to affect women in different and often conflicting ways. Discrimination under the law and at work, allied to the problem of surplus women, fuelled support for a movement that seemed to offer the hope of change and improvement in women's social and political situation. Yet at the same time other factors encouraged the traditional sex roles. Concern over the national stock, the Empire and perceived military threats furthered the notion that political power did indeed rest on physical force. Again, any possible challenge to the roles of men and women had to be opposed: 'For obvious reasons' one anti-suffragist claimed 'nature has assigned to men the duty of providing sustenance for the family, and to the woman the administration of the home' (Page 1912), while the Women's National League for Opposing Women's Suffrage agreed that 'the natural vocation of women is marriage and the family, not the mill' (*WNLOWS* October 2, 1908). In fact the whole women's suffrage movement had to be opposed because 'it cuts down to the roots of our family life . . . and could lead to anarchy in the home' (*WNLOWS* nd–c.1908).

Was the women's suffrage movement a single issue campaign or was it a wider assault on male power and stereotyped sex roles? Certainly the infamous 'anti' Sir Almroth E. Wright feared it was the latter. He argued that women's biology made them inferior to men and that suffragism would upset this natural balance. Indeed, 'the failure to recognise that man is master, and why he is master, lies at the root of Women's Suffrage' (Wright 1913:71). He was also worried that 'the women's suffrage that leads to feminism would be a social disaster' (*ibid.*:68).

Although votes for women faced considerable parliamentary obstacles, perhaps these sentiments reflected the true basis of the opposition to suffragism: after all, the very fact of organising and acting together as women explicitly attacked many cherished notions of the capabilities of the 'fair sex' during a period when maternal and domestic roles were being particularly emphasised. Yet, in fact, a major part of the suffragists' ideological heritage was based on an acceptance of these roles. And, at the same time, the values of the political structure to which the suffragists demanded access were being seriously challenged. How did the major suffragist societies react to this complex scene?

FOR THESE WE FIGHT.

ʌo. 2—The Wife.

WIFE: "John! Where's the rest of your twenty-five shillings? How am I going to pay the landlord, and buy food for the children?"

HUSBAND: (*who has just thrown two shillings and sixpence on the table*): "Shut up! What I do with my money is no business of yours."

"SUPPORTED" BY HER HUSBAND.

"A man works from sun to sun, A woman's work is never done."

Cartoons from the WSPU paper, The Vote
Above: February 24 1911. Below: July 21 1911

Suffragette postcard. By courtesy of the Director and Board of Governors of the Museum of London

2 The National Union of Women's Suffrage Societies

In her reply to me she said 'I know the Women's Freedom League and have heard of the WSPU but who in the world are the Constitutionals?' I have taken this reproof to heart and have not yet become a 'baa lamb'.

(Letter to *The Vote* November 18, 1909)

The 'non-militant' NUWSS was the largest organisation that fought for votes for women. It was set up just before the turn of the century although its origins can be traced to the campaign to secure a women's suffrage amendment to the 1866 Reform Bill. Suffrage societies in London and Manchester were formed at that time to press the issue and, despite disputes, the movement grew, resulting in the birth of the NUWSS in 1897 (Blackburn 1902). By 1909 the National Union had 70 affiliated societies with 13,161 members and its growth forced a reorganisation on a federal basis in the same year. In 1914 membership reached over 53,000 with 480 affiliated societies (NUWSS Annual Reports). It was a democratic organisation with an elected president, Millicent Garrett Fawcett, and a national executive committee. Policy was decided by the membership through annual, or occasionally bi-annual, conferences. The Union was strictly legal in its methods and its aim was 'to obtain the Parliamentary Franchise for women on the same terms as it is or may be granted to men' (*The Common Cause* April 18, 1910).

Although democratic, the development of the Union was not without its problems. It had in fact been born partly out of a disagreement among suffragists over the affiliation of other organisations, and, in time, Millicent Fawcett was accused of autocracy, particularly during the First World War. However, in spite of internal friction, the NUWSS was important by virtue of its size and democratic structure; it was much more likely to respond to and to reflect the needs of women than was the autocratic WSPU. Furthermore, although well-known Tories (such as Lady Chance) and Liberals (such as Millicent Fawcett) were prominent in the National Union, others, notably Clementina Black and Isabella O. Ford, had long associations with the socialist and Labour movements and served on the Executive Committee. Furthermore, the voice of working class women, through the societies representing the industrial North, was increasingly heard: this had important strategic and theoretical implications that again suggest the inaccuracy of the traditional image of the 'non-militant' suffragists. Women like Selina Cooper and Ada Nield Chew were no 'baa lambs' (Liddington and Norris 1978; Nield Chew 1982).

The feminist debate within the National Union was reflected in its national literature and, in particular, in its paper *The Common Cause* (first issue April 15, 1909). The Union had contributed to *The Women's Franchise*, but its growth demanded that it have its own weekly paper, edited by Helena Swanwick (1909–1912), Clementina Black (1912–1913) and Agnes Maude Royden. A wide variety of opinions was expressed within the paper, essential reading for any student of suffragism. Although its prime aim was, of course, to push for the vote, Helena Swanwick, for example, felt that the paper's role was to 'publish articles and news which would show the many sides in which life touches women and the many ways in which the subjection of women reacts upon life' (*Cause* April 14, 1910). Although more local studies of suffragism are required, it is clear that *The Common Cause* became a crucial element in the expression of suffragist thought.

In 1911, before the second reading of the Conciliation Bill which would have enfranchised some women, *The Common Cause* published, on its front page, a rather rustic drawing of a female reaper gathering corn. On this idyllic scene was inscribed the motto 'Faith, Perseverance and Patience' (*Cause* March 30, 1911). These were qualities the NUWSS enjoyed in abundance: perseverance and patience throughout the long battle from 1867 to 1918, and then to 1928, but most of all Faith – in the power of the vote. Women's suffrage would lead to higher wages and economic independence (*Cause* May 5, 1910:52; Royden 1911), increased job opportunities (Shillington 1909:2–3), improved marriages and child welfare (*Cause* October, 7, 1909:339; August 26, 1909:250), legal equality (McLaren 1908:36–7), and so much more. In short, the vote would ultimately improve women's position and its effect 'would be subtle, gradual and far reaching . . . tremendous and beneficent to the relations between men and women' (*Cause* February 24, 1910:639).

However limited the value of the vote may now seem, it must be emphasised that the struggle of the suffragists – an active struggle by women, as women – was at the time controversial. It aroused the opposition not only of men who felt that a woman's place was in the home, but also of those frightened of any possible progress towards adult suffrage (Harrison 1978:33). This fear existed even though the suffragist demand for the vote on the same terms as men meant, in effect, that not all women would be enfranchised even if it were granted. Not all men had the vote (Blewitt 1972), and Millicent Fawcett's policy throughout (and right up to 1918) seems to have been that half a loaf was better than none.

What these suffragist arguments can be seen to have implied is that the contemporary political structure, with the obvious suffrage reform, could have met and satisfied women's demands. And, further, what other suffragist arguments can be seen to have implied is that these demands could also be met without major changes in women's domestic and maternal roles. Indeed, according to a particular strand of liberal feminism, society was unbalanced because the sex-bound character-istics and virtues of women were not politically represented. It was an argument based on an acceptance of the 'natural' sexual division of labour. As Millicent Fawcett wrote:

To women as mothers is given the charge of the home and the care of children. Women are therefore, by nature as well as training and occupation, more accustomed than men to concentrate their minds on the home and the domestic side of things . . . I want to see the womanly and domestic side of things weigh more and count more in all public concerns.

(Fawcett 1905)

Others argued that 'Home is the sphere of woman . . . By voting a woman would not give up one jot or tittle of her womanliness or care for the home' (*Women's Franchise* July 11, 1907:23); and 'women wanted the vote because they wanted to improve the homes of the country' (*ibid*. August 8, 1907:70). While these attitudes, given the ideological heritage of suffragism and the contemporary pressures on women, were not surprising, they did indicate a basic contradiction: how could there be equal opportunities for all women if their natural function was in the home?

Although the feminist debate within the National Union quickly began to expand, this type of argument, based on the contemporary division of the 'natural' differences of the sexes and their associated roles, was common. The very first issue of *The Common Cause* was keen to point out that

it is the notion that women's suffrage means the breaking up of the home, the causing of domestic strife, the setting of women against men, that the very name of this paper is intended to deny . . . the mother half of humanity should be given its proper place . . . the temperate, affectional woman nature, intent on the conservation of the home and race should have its due beside the more extreme male and appetitive nature.

(*Cause* April 15, 1909:3)

The paper also agreed with the 'antis' who 'cry "Women's sphere is in the home" but in addition we say "Give us the power to keep them in the home". This is one of the many reasons why women want the vote' (*ibid*. May 27, 1909:93).

Votes were also what women working outside the home needed.

Although increasingly responsive to working class women, it appears that, in the national literature at least, the Union felt little could be done to ameliorate their position without the vote. The NUWSS pressed this point at the 1908 National Union of Women Workers' Conference (Executive Committee Minutes June 4, 1908), and other members agreed that 'until women have votes their trade unions and other organisations can do little to help them because they do not have the political power which has made men's unions so valuable to them'; and that 'it requires only a little thought to understand how the wages of women workers are suffering today because they do not have the vote' (Shillington 1909:2). A. Maude Royden, in her *Votes and Wages: How Women's Suffrage Will Improve the Economic Position of Women* (1911), went further and claimed that the vote would not only increase wages but would open more trades, lead to better conditions and stop 'sweated' work as well. At no time, however, did the National Union declare trade unionism for women to be worthless.

Limited as this early approach may now appear, care has to be taken in its evaluation. First, suffragists could argue that calls for wider opportunities for women, alongside an acceptance of women's 'natural' interests, were not necessarily contradictory – what they were demanding for women was a choice. Secondly, the range of feminist arguments was already widening by 1910. Helena Swanwick, for example, criticised the notion that 'women are to exist merely for the propagation of the race and for the enjoyment of man', and argued that they would never be 'happy and self respecting . . . until they are free; free to bear children or not; free to work and free to determine the laws under which they must live' (*Cause* April 14, 1910:3). Elsewhere, marriage as it stood was attacked as 'a lottery' (*ibid.* May 12, 1910:68), while support was given to married women workers (*ibid.* September 9, 1909:74). In this connection, a call was also made for nurseries along with 'cheap restaurants, so that nursing mothers might have their own dinner when they come to give the baby its dinner' (*ibid.* June 17, 1909:125).

The growing fluidity of the feminist debate within the NUWSS was perhaps best reflected in Lady McLaren's *Women's Charter of Rights and Liberties* (1910; see Appendix I). The Charter's proposals were never formally adopted by the National Union (although Lady McLaren was herself a suffragist), but they were evidently discussed (*Cause* March 17; March 24; June 30, 1910). The Charter had apparently arisen out of the 1909 meeting of the International Women's Suffrage Alliance and was, in many ways, a classic example of a particular strand of suffragist feminism. The author went beyond the usual calls for improvements in the law and the vote by demanding, for example, wages for housework, the recognition of childcare as work and a system of communal services for women.

The great majority of wives are devoting their time to unpaid work, and when the importance of the work is considered, it appears extraordinary that the services of wives have no money value placed on them . . . a wife who works diligently and devotedly to the family service should be entitled to such wages of a servant or housekeeper as are usual in that station of life in which she lives and this in addition to her board.

(McLaren 1910:10)

Not only should women's work in the home be paid, but 'as women devote so much of their time to the unpaid work of rearing children' this should be recognised too (*ibid.*:20). These radical proposals were perhaps still based on a sexual division of labour, yet Lady McLaren did write of an ideal system where women had 'a share in the home life and a share in the independence of the wage earner', aided 'by the creche, the public kitchen and the public wash house' (*ibid.*:33). Finally she argued that 'until the economic independence of women is secured in all countries so long will the tale of women's suffering and misery continue. The girl who is not economically independent is not free' (*ibid.*:58).

Yet Lady McLaren – like many suffragists – never explained how economic independence for all women was to be achieved. Moreover, as well as accepting the political structure, her proposals were based on the notion that housework and childcare were indeed solely the responsibility of women. (Elsewhere she writes of the need for domestic schools – for women and girls only.) Nonetheless, the Charter remains a remarkable document – fully appreciating the arduous work of many women and suggesting some valuable reforms. It was reprinted in *The Common Cause* (March 17, 1910:691) and clearly reflected the widening discussion within the NUWSS from 1910 onwards.

There were several reasons for the expansion of the debate within the National Union. The growth of the Union after 1909 (for reasons outlined in the previous chapter) was clearly important, as was the unwillingness of many women to join the WSPU. Although the Pankhursts certainly kept the issue of votes for women alive, their autocracy and ever more desperate tactics drove more women into the 'non-militant' camp. Here, the democratic structure of the National Union, aided by the reorganisation of 1909, allowed the voice of many more women to be heard. But the most important reason why the boundaries of the feminist debate widened was the growing identification of the NUWSS with the Labour movement and with working class women. This must be considered in some detail as it not only challenges the orthodox view of women's suffrage as simply 'bourgeois', but has other strategic and ideological implications.

Liddington and Norris (1978) have already shown that, for Lancashire working women at least, women's suffrage was not just a middle class concern. Suffragist activists there had strong links with the Independent Labour Party (ILP) and trade union circles, and their demand for the vote was linked to the needs of working women. Radical suffragists, like Esther Roper and Eva Gore-Booth, in fact wanted the whole suffrage movement to have a wider social base and a much stronger association with working class women. It was a call that met an increasingly warm response within the NUWSS, especially after 1909.

The fate of the struggle at Westminster was a crucial factor in the growing radicalism of the National Union. From 1910 onwards the 'Faith, Perseverance and Patience' of the NUWSS leadership was sorely tested. It had pinned its hopes on the Conciliation Bills of 1910 and 1911 but these were doomed without Government support. Millicent Fawcett accepted Asquith's promise of a Reform Bill capable of including a women's amendment (*Cause* November 23, 1911:569), and criticised both the WSPU's scepticism of this offer and its return, after intermittent truces, to militancy. For once it seems that the WSPU was right since the Speaker ruled a women's suffrage amendment to the Reform Bill out of order in January 1913. The NUWSS was furious. 'The broad fact is that for suffragists the parliamentary machine has broken down', *The Common Cause* declared, 'and the Commons have proved themselves once more a body impotent to translate their opinions into law' (January 31, 1913:733). While the Union refused to accept or condone the militant tactics of the WSPU, its ridicule of the Commons and Parliament as a whole was biting. Complaining of 'the singular emptiness and unreality of the procedure in the House of Commons', the Union continued that, to people with a genuine grasp of reality, 'the gentlemen of that assembly present themselves too often as schoolboys solemnly obeying the rules of an intricate game and believing – as cricketers appear to do – that the issues of their sport are of concern to the world and their contemporary captain among the elect of the earth' (*ibid.* February 7, 1913:752).

While all this took place at a time when parliamentary democracy appeared to be under growing attack, the NUWSS nonetheless remained a suffragist body and, in its very demand for votes, implicitly confirmed its belief in liberal democracy. And, although it concentrated its vitriolic criticism on the headmaster and his pupils rather than on the school itself, the frustration at the lack of parliamentary progress after 1910 was instrumental in the sharpening of both the political and the feminist analyses of the Union. Most importantly of all, the continuing failure to gain any measure of votes for women further convinced the national leadership of the need for a mass campaign and for a closer alliance with the Labour movement.

This alliance, under its Election Fighting Fund (EFF) policy, actually began in the middle of 1912 (Special Council Meeting NUWSS

May 14/15, 1912). It was particularly unique for it had overcome two formidable obstacles – the non-party tradition of the NUWSS and the debate over women's suffrage in the Labour Party. The argument in the Labour Party was between those who were fully committed to adult suffrage and others, such as Hardie, who would accept even a limited bill for women. The adult suffragists thus accused their opponents of favouring a policy that would benefit only propertied women. There were many acrimonious debates within the party over this issue – an issue which made the position of radical suffragists particularly difficult. Nonetheless, the dilemma was resolved, for in 1912 the Party Conference declared that 'no bill can be acceptable to the Labour and Socialist Movement which does not include women' (*Cause* February 1, 1912). By 1913 the TUC had adopted a similar policy, too (*ibid.* September 12, 1913).

This change in Labour's official line on women's suffrage led to a fundamental shift in the electoral policy of the NUWSS. Previously it had supported loyal friends of women's suffrage but now, with one or two exceptions, it officially supported Labour candidates as the representatives of the only party committed to votes for women. They were to be actively and financially supported through the Election Fighting Fund. Such candidates were, technically, to be supported on suffrage grounds only and the official line was that 'it would not be a departure from the non-party attitude of the Union; moreover it would not be an alliance between the NUWSS and the Labour Party' (*ibid.* May 23, 1912). Officially then, it was presented as a purely strategic move to pressurise the Liberals. Ramsay McDonald probably saw it in this way. By no means a feminist, he believed, however, that women's suffrage would, in the long run, benefit Labour (Morgan 1975:129).

Despite the official line of the National Union, some members found it impossible to accept the new policy. They opposed this startling departure from the old 'non-party' position at the Special Council Meeting in May 1912. Other members were concerned that the new policy would lead the NUWSS to support Labour at the next General Election, scheduled for 1915. Such was the concern over the EFF that four members of the National Executive Committee, including Eleanor Rathbone and Margaret Corbett Ashby, formed an inner circle to oppose it (NUWSS Executive Committee Minutes March 5, 1914). Millicent Fawcett was furious, accusing them of endangering the very existence of the Union, and they resigned in May 1914 (*ibid.* March 19; May 7, 1914).

Millicent Fawcett herself supported the new policy for tactical reasons rather than through a desire to associate the Union with socialism. She argued that, after the failure of 1911, only a Government Bill would succeed and that Asquith would only be moved if suffragism had and was seen to have widespread support (see chapter 7). Furthermore, in view of the imminent General Election, the Prime Minister would have to consider the potential threat of Labour. The EFF was designed to increase that worry. As one EFF pamphlet (1914) put it,

In the constituencies . . . Liberalism and Conservatism are today threatened by Labour, and the central fact of the times which are ahead of us is the rapidly extending association of the workers with the political aims of women . . . And, if Ministerial organisers will permit a not unfriendly word they will think less of the suffragists who depend on physical force . . . and more [of] the suffragists [who] are in every direction reinforcing Labour and influencing the balancing vote on which depends the fates of Governments.

Nonetheless, and however much it was denied, a large body of support for the EFF came from women who did want a broader association with the Labour Party. In any case, it would be difficult to isolate the wider political views of organisers like Ada Nield Chew and Selina Cooper from the policy of supporting Labour candidates on suffrage grounds alone. That this was taking place was reflected in the executive's repeated demand that 'speeches and writings in support of EFF candidates shall . . . base that support on women's suffrage grounds only' (NUWSS Executive Committee Minutes June 5, 1913; May 7, 1914).

It is difficult to see how this could have effectively worked in practice. Even the National Union's own paper, *The Common Cause*, was, from 1912 onwards claiming that the whole basis of the suffragists' demand rested on working class women. Hardie's *Labour Leader* and the Labour *Daily Citizen* were recommended to readers (*Cause* July 18, 1912:243; July 25, 1912:265) and frontispieces such as that showing a working class family reflected the Union's wider support of the Labour movement (*ibid.* May 16, 1912). That the Union was now basing its demands on the position of working class women was made absolutely clear when *The Common Cause* reprinted an 'excellent' letter from the longstanding socialist, Isabella O. Ford, to the *Daily Citizen* which pointed out that

All the Women's Suffrage Societies now fully realise that the unjust position of working women is at the very root of our demand . . . I can speak with the most intimate knowledge of the National Union on this point, for I have always been a member. Our demand has never been for the propertied.

(*Cause* January 3, 1913:671)

The creation of the Election Fighting Fund could be seen as a purely strategic development although in some ways it was a continuation of a process that had begun before 1912. In 1910 alone the Union had supported, amongst others, the women chainmakers in Cradley Heath (*ibid.* September 8; September 15, 1910:350) and striking women

The Common Cause

THE ORGAN OF THE NATIONAL UNION OF

Women's Suffrage

Societies

Vol. IV. No. 162.

May 16th, 1912.

1D.

The Common Cause,

The Organ of the National Union of

Women's Suffrage

Societies.

MARCH 30, 1911.

One Penny.

Vol. II. No. 103.

ENGLAND SCOTLAND IRELAND & WALES · NATIONAL UNION OF WOMEN'S SUFFRAGE SOCIETIES

FAITH · PERSEVERANCE · PATIENCE

A WEAPON OF OPPRESSION.

The honourable badge of marriage becomes a weapon of oppression if any point to it to excuse the under-payment of women workers.

Employer (Skirt-maker) to Employee: Here, there's too much coming out your side.

printers in Edinburgh (*ibid.*: September 15, 1910:365). In 1911 it supported the wives of striking port workers in Manchester (*ibid.* July 13, 1911:242) and the right of the Pit Brow women to continue working in the coalfields (*ibid.* August 10, 1911:313). It was also making increasingly warm references to the Labour Party before 1912.

Throughout this period, although still firmly committed to the vote, both the language and the political analysis of a major part of the Union began to change. For example, *The Common Cause* now wrote of the need for a redistribution of wealth (May 16, 1912:82) and increasingly linked the suffrage cause with that of the Labour movement. It also began to publish radical cartoons. One, for example, illustrated how employers extracted surplus value from their workers (July 31, 1914:351); another, 'A Weapon of Oppression', encouraged women to join trade unions while bitterly attacking the underpayment of married women workers (May 29, 1914:165).

Overall the NUWSS certainly became identified with the cause of working women and the Labour Party, however much the latter connection may be denied. What else could Asquith believe when Miss Robertson, a member of an official NUWSS delegation, declared to him that

working men have come to regard this not as a sex question but as a democratic one. They think their class should have more representation and have begun to identify Anti-Suffragism with the war of capital against labour . . . The Trade Unions . . . believe that opposition [to votes for women] comes from capitalists who want women cheap . . . the Unions are increasingly determined that the women must be enfranchised.

(*Cause* August 15, 1913:319)

And, finally, while much has been made of Asquith's reply to a deputation from Sylvia Pankhurst in June 1914 (he implied that if women were to have the vote, this would have to be on a wide basis), the campaign of the NUWSS from 1910 onwards was equally, if not more, crucial (see chapter 7).

Although the NUWSS never adopted a socialist analysis its growth and democratic organisation, alongside strategic considerations, had led it to a position which implied that the struggle for emancipation went beyond the vote and was linked to class. Moreover, although the old strands of feminism remained, new and more radical ideas emerged. This process culminated in 1914 and was perhaps best illustrated by the articles written by Ada Nield Chew, a radical suffragist from Lancashire and a full-time organiser for the Union from 1911 to 1914 (Nield Chew 1982).

In the first of these articles, 'The Problem of Married Working Women', Ada Nield Chew pushed back the boundaries of suffragist feminism by attacking 'the ideal of the domestic tabby cat woman as that to which all womanhood should aspire'. She criticised middle class women for still claiming it was 'the noblest and only legitimate sphere' open to women and argued further that 'women are no more fit for domestic tasks or for baby tending than all men are fit to be engineers'. In fact, she added, it was cruel 'to compel women who have no gift for child care to spend their lives in doing endless rounds of domestic jobs and looking after their babies in the intervals' (*Cause* February 27, 1919:910).

This amounted to a clear attack on the suffragist argument that was based on the acceptance of the sexual division of labour. It came from a woman with a lifetime of experience in the organisation of working women, and one who realised that the vote was not enough.

The bondage of the married working woman is twofold; the dependence of her young children, and the primitive state in which domestic drudgery remains. In other words her babies and her domestic jobs are the chains which bind her and it is these chains which must be broken before talk of human development becomes more than just talk.

(*Cause* March 6, 1914:933)

Finally, clearly aiming her remarks at the more traditional suffragist, Ada Nield Chew argued:

Slaves should break their chains and they who want women to be free should help in the chain breaking and not try to rivet the links closer by advocating domestic teaching for all schools for all girls, fostering in the minds of girls that simply because of their sex they must inevitably some day be ready to cook a man's dinner and tidy up his hearth.

(*ibid.*)

While this implied a wider vision of emancipation, it would be mistaken to see Ada Nield Chew's ideas as dominant within the NUWSS as a whole. The two articles quoted above were prefaced by a statement that they did not necessarily represent the policy of the Union, and both articles were immediately attacked by another contributor to *The Common Cause*, Edith Chattle (*ibid.* March 13, 1914:952). Meanwhile, the notions that a woman is 'naturally best qualified to deal with the problems which concern the home, the mother and the child' (*Parliament and The Children*, NUWSS 1913), and that the 'home is her unalienable sphere' (*Cause* August 22, 1912:340) were still common. Indeed, in *Why Homekeeping Women Want The Vote* (NUWSS 1913), it was argued that

A lot of people say 'A woman's sphere is in the home'. If by this they mean that in most cases where a man marries, he has to go on working outside the home while she stays in it in order to look after it and all that is in it, *I think we all agree about this*. But suffragists think that it is because women think so much of their homes and care so much about them, that they ought to have votes.

Thus, although the debate after 1910 showed how radical some of the 'non-militants' could be, there was still a strong current of opinion within the Union that accepted both the political structure and the idea of the woman's sphere. This could be regarded as contradictory, but it could also be seen as a reflection of the vitality of the discussion within the Union. Throughout this discussion, the oppression that countless working women faced was continually condemned. As M.S. Reeves in her 'Wife of The Working Man' put it,

Between bearing, nursing and rearing children; scrubbing, sweeping and clean-ing rooms; washing, ironing and mending clothes; cooking, serving and clear-ing away meals, the labourer's wife lives a life of such extraordinary toil that only the most certain and brilliant future would explain equal devotion in a free human being. But all her ceaseless activity brings her no security, no prospects . . . She is, when all is said and done, a kept woman.

(*Cause* February 6, 1914:833–4)

Views of motherhood, sex and birth control were, understandably perhaps, restrained. Indeed, the tremendous contemporary pressures on women to become mothers usually elicited what seems to have been a traditional response. Thus, woman's duty to the Empire was appar-ently accepted (*The Question of the Moment: The Real Issue of Women's Suffrage*, NUWSS 1912), as was the natural role of mother and child-carer, with the implication that women would be better mothers once they had the vote. However, the Union was well aware of the disparity between the ideal and the reality of motherhood. Helena Swanwick, for example, complained bitterly of the 'hideous' conditions in which many women, especially working women, had their children. She argued, too, that many women were forced into motherhood against their will and that they suffered a growing threat from the spread of venereal disease (*Cause* September 8, 1910:351). Whether or not this justified criticism of the reality of motherhood challenged the idea that a woman's role was, after all, in the home looking after children, is debatable. Ada Nield Chew's views were by no means predominant.

Related to motherhood were, of course, the crucial issues of repro-duction and sexuality. How could women enjoy equal opportunities if reproduction was controlled by men? More controversially, were men alone allowed to have a sexuality unconnected with procreation? Although women in the NUWSS were well aware of the importance of this issue, it is understandable that public discussion was limited. Tactically, the National Union's leadership was keen to avoid any accusations of immorality (Millicent Fawcett once refused to share a platform with Edward Carpenter for this reason), and the growing concern over the spread of venereal disease further tempered any proposals for sexual liberation. Most importantly, the contemporary moral code was still strong and, all things considered, it was not surprising that many women adopted the apparent safety of mono-gamous marriage and the demand, not for a change in the moral ideal, but that men also live up to it.

Thus references to contraception, 'A very controversial subject, and one on which much may be said' (*ibid*. November 7, 1913:537) were extremely rare. Nonetheless *The Common Cause* once declared, without going into details, that 'thoughtful women all over the country are beginning to feel that it would be far more in harmony with a higher ideal of life to produce fewer children and rear them in health and strength to live' (August 26, 1909:250). It once, very quietly, even recommended a publication entitled *Marriage and Motherhood. A Wives' Handbook*, which outlined the available methods of birth control (*ibid*. December 1913:618). At the same time, an awareness of the results of unwanted pregnancies was clearly evident. One article told of a pregnant woman who had 14 children and had asked a doctor for an abortion, adding that 'women are placed in such sex slavery when they marry that the mistress is often safer than the wife. They may be forced to bear children against their will' (*ibid*. September 8, 1910:351).

The public discussion of sex was muted, too, although the Union was clearly willing to criticise sexual oppression. Yet this criticism was based on the moral ideal and on the accepted assumption that, in Louisa Martindale's words, sex was something which 'Nature had given women for the propagation of the race only' (Martindale 1910:70). In fact, the belief that the women's suffrage movement was part of a moral crusade was prevalent. 'The question of sex morality,' Lady Chance wrote, 'lies deep at the root of the Women's Suffrage question . . . [but] We want to make everybody feel that it is equally wrong for both sexes to transgress the moral law. The Women's Movement is in fact a great moral movement' (Chance 1913:8).

Many suffragists argued for the safety of chastity and monogamy, and condemned the sexual hypocrisy of men; the two positions were linked. For example, *The Common Cause* argued that venereal disease was responsible for the sterility of many married women and for nearly half of infant mortality (*Cause* September 8, 1910:352). If this had been true, or even believed to be true, it is hardly surprising that the Union did not call for greater sexual freedom. On the whole, however, despite the occasional plea for sex education for children and brides (*ibid*. December 13, 1912:618; June 5, 1914:193) the Union's attitude left the values of the moral code unquestioned. The solution to the sexual oppression of women was seen as the vote (Chance 1913:7).

From a study of the years 1914–18 it is difficult to speculate as to whether or not the National Union would have become more radical –

even perhaps in its attitude towards sex and morality – had not the War intervened. Certainly, the NUWSS was becoming increasingly progressive. For example, the logic of its political strategy was such that it would surely have supported the Labour Party in the General Election scheduled for 1915. However, the War years do illustrate some important characteristics of the suffragism of the NUWSS.

In the first place, despite Millicent Fawcett's support for the War, the NUWSS never adopted the extreme jingoism of the WSPU, and it continued to protect and push the interests of women. It involved itself in relief work throughout the War and set up a Personal Liberties Committee in January 1915 'for watching over the interests of women during the war especially with regard to infringements of personal liberties' (Minutes January 1, 1915). The Union also warned in 1915 of the 'danger that in their eagerness to perform some national service the very women who are in the best position to demand adequate wages and better conditions may neglect these considerations, thus . . . an opportunity of raising the status of women workers will be lost' (*Cause* August 6, 1915:229). Although suffrage activity was originally suspended, it was resumed in late 1916, and the Union was very active in pressing the Speaker's Conference of 1917 to adopt some measure of votes for women.

In spite of such positive attitudes, the War led to a serious split within the NUWSS which, in 1915, looked almost on the point of collapse. The crisis was, on the surface, the result of conflicting views over what the Union's policy concerning the War should be. Millicent Fawcett regretted, but did not reject, the War and expressed the hope in August 1914 that as women '[we] show ourselves worthy of citizenship, whether our claim to it be recognised or not' (*ibid.* August 14, 1914:385). Many other women had hoped the Union would campaign for peace, and were critical of the president's apparently pro-War stance. They supported successful motions at the February Annual Council meeting which called for an educational campaign on the causes and the results of war. Another motion, which could be interpreted as a call for a negotiated peace, was also carried. Significantly this stated that 'since the Women's Suffrage movement is based on the principle that social relations should be governed not by physical force but by recognition of mutual rights this Council of the NUWSS declares its belief in Arbitration as opposed to war' (*ibid.* February 12, 1915:711). These were not calls for peace at any price, and some pacifists, for example Kathleen Courtenay and Catherine Marshall, resigned because the calls did not go far enough (Newberry 1977:418).

But there were also mass resignations as a result of Millicent Fawcett's identification of the NUWSS with a pro-War policy and her interpretation of the motions passed in February. During the Council meeting she argued that there could be no peace until the Germans were out of France and Holland: 'Until that is done, I believe it is akin to treason to talk of peace' (Strachey 1931:288). This was clearly aimed at those 'pacifist' members of the National Executive Committee who were deeply shocked by their president's statement. In the following weeks it became clear that Millicent Fawcett's opposition to sending delegates to the forthcoming International Women's Suffrage Conference (a truce and a negotiated peace were on the agenda) and her jingoistic statements made their position untenable, so that famous and longstanding Union members such as Isabella O. Ford, Helena Swanwick and Margaret Ashton resigned along with other members of the Executive Committee and all the officers except the treasurer (*ibid.*:290). They refused to stand again at the Special Half Yearly Council in June where the president managed, with the support of the smaller rural societies, to push through her policy. Strachey argued that 'the feeling in the Union was strongly behind her' (*ibid.*:291) but this is debatable; most of the 'pacifist' support came from the large societies in industrial areas. It was as if she had 'called in the old world to redress the balance of the new' (Morgan 1975:136).

The crisis revealed the power and influence of Millicent Garrett Fawcett – it is suspicious that the Executive Committee minutes for June 1914 to February 1915 have long been missing. The split also suggests that the pre-War radicalism of the NUWSS was seen by some as purely strategic, to be used to frighten the Liberals. Certainly, Millicent Fawcett's patriotism and attitude to the War denied the class analysis that appeared to be developing up to 1914, and led, for example, to the suspension of the Election Fighting Fund because of the ILP's association with pacifism. Even *The Common Cause* argued that 'Great Britain has gone to war. This is a British paper. We accept the war' (August 14, 1914:386). The president of the NUWSS (who had in fact supported an appeal for peace in August 1914) could reply that any tinge of pacifism might endanger the essential success of the suffrage campaign, but her pro-War stance surely went beyond strategic considerations.

Indeed, the critics of Mrs Fawcett claimed that she had betrayed suffragism and all that it stood for. Many women felt that suffragism was rooted in notions of democratic equality which argued that power was not, or should not be, based on physical force, as the 'antis' claimed. This essentially liberal position condemned the War as resulting from a world made by men and as contrary to true suffragist and democratic principles, and was a major factor behind the demand for the NUWSS to campaign for peace and arbitration. In a sad, private circular explaining her resignation from the National Executive and the Manchester Federation, Margaret Ashton stated that the ideal behind the Union was one of co-operation between men and women working for the rule of right over might. The NUWSS had thus 'failed us in our hour of need', and this had been due to 'a failing of leadership that has left so many members untouched by the real meaning of the whole women's movement of which the vote is only one part' (Ashton 1915). However, both Margaret Ashton's letter and Millicent Fawcett's action indicated the conservative limits of a major part of the suffragism of the NUWSS as compared with Sylvia Pankhurst's revolutionary analysis of the War.

Although, as mentioned above, the National Union actively tried to protect women and organise relief work during the War, significantly, the radical feminism of 1914 did not re-emerge within *The Common Cause* or other national literature. The Union did maintain some links with the Labour movement: the NUWSS continued to back trade unionism for women. It condemned, too, profiteering by unscrupulous employers (*Cause* April 23, 1915:25), and some wide-ranging views on the role of women were still expressed: on the one hand, Dr H. Wilson argued in late 1914 that 'the most precious national service that women can render, in peace or war, is the care of the home, the guardianship of the family' (*ibid.* November 20, 1914:551); while, two years later, a Union pamphlet argued that the War had 'brought great publicity to women's work, with the result that the tradition that women's only place is in the home has disappeared' (*A Memorandum* . . ., NUWSS 1916:5).

Ultimately, however, even some of the more radical proposals made during the War have to be carefully analysed. For example, there were repeated calls for co-operative housekeeping in order to release women for War service (*Cause* September 8, 1916:276), but these were based on the assumption that housework was still essentially women's work. Similarly, the granting of state allowances to mothers was demanded with the War in mind (*ibid.* June 23, 1916:143), and implied that childcare was women's natural forte. Both proposals at least recognised these traditional roles as work, but they did little to challenge the assumption that they were 'natural' functions of women. Moreover, when the NUWSS started to re-agitate for the vote after the War, most arguments were based on an acceptance of the separate spheres. Women needed the vote since, when peace came, many of the problems to be solved were 'to do with the home and children' (*Women and The Nation*, NUWSS 1917). After all, should not 'the hand that rocks the cradle . . . help to rule the world?' (*Women Workers*, NUWSS 1917).

The NUWSS resumed its suffragist work when it became clear that a new electoral register was necessary. It held huge meetings with women workers (*Cause* March 2, 1917:623) and began its propaganda work again. The Union was quite willing to use the war work argument, claiming that 'Women have shown in every phase of national life, that they can stand with and beside their men in taking up the national responsibility. This is the supreme test for citizenship – and the vote is the recognition of the citizen's status' (*ibid*. October 26, 1916:350). However, the pre-War identification with working class women had gone. Significantly, most of the ardent supporters of the EFF had either left the Union in the split of 1915 or were disillusioned by its position over the War.

Yet the leadership of the NUWSS argued publicly that the struggle was not over even with the passing of the Representation of the People Act in 1918. It criticised the age restriction and continued to demand equal rights as reflected in its change of name, in 1919, to the National Union of Societies for Equal Citizenship. It complained 'that the idea of equal opportunities for men and women has not been fulfilled. The enfranchisement of women is not a matter of the vote alone . . . until we have a world in which there are no sex barriers . . . the purpose of the Suffragists will not be fulfilled' (*ibid*. January 25, 1918:531). Yet, to all intents and purposes, it seemed that the Union's aim had been achieved, and membership declined after 1918.

Although suffragists got the vote in 1918 this was in many ways a limited victory. Women's war work may have changed some attitudes but it was by no means the only factor. The War had removed many of the political obstacles (for example, an 'anti' Prime Minister) to women's suffrage, and both Labour and Liberal were now keen to attract the new voters. But, although the pre-War suffrage campaign itself cannot be discounted, in some respects little had changed: the age limit reflected a fear of a majority of female voters, and the suffrage came when, under the Defence of the Realm Act (DORA), the Government were still restricting the movement of women in military areas. The attitudes of the state had changed little: in its attempt to curb venereal disease, under DORA, any woman suspected of prostitution could be picked up off the streets and forced to undergo a medical examination.

The National Union's struggle for the vote had raised many feminist and political issues, particularly in the years leading up to the War. There was a closer relationship with the Labour movement and a more progressive feminist analysis. Millicent Fawcett may have supported the Election Fighting Fund policy on strategic grounds only, but this further associated the NUWSS with the problems of working class women. And while some arguments may now appear limited, given the contemporary pressures on women, they were still remarkable in their identification of many aspects of women's oppression. Even those suffragists whose arguments rested on an acceptance of 'woman's sphere' at least could argue that they were calling for a choice. Yet ultimately that choice was restricted, for it seemed that women's biology 'naturally' led them into childcare and the home. Clearly a major component of suffragist feminism, as represented by the NUWSS, was based on this idea and it prevented a fundamental analysis of sex role stereotyping and of a woman's role in the family from emerging. Indeed, as Millicent Fawcett wrote to Asquith, 'women are . . . in a special degree the guardian of the home and family, a fact recognised by suffragists and anti-suffragists alike' (September 13, 1913).

Politically, the National Union's demand for the vote implied that emancipation could have come through a reform of the political structure, rather than through its complete transformation. Although some women, both in and out of the suffrage movement, were critical of either position, such ideas certainly appeared to be central to suffragist thinking. However, many more local studies of the National Union, which represented over 50,000 women by 1914, are required before a definitive view can be taken.

3 The Women's Freedom League

We yielded concession after concession in order to satisfy those who wanted to get power within the movement by other means than by sheer devotion and hard work, but all the power that they had obtained by this concession only made them stronger to spread disaffection and disruption in the ranks . . . There are disappointed place seekers and those who have no thought but that they were more capable of filling certain posts than those who have been selected. The seceding camp is made up of every dissatisfied and disappointed person and is held together by no bonds of union such as the bonds which unite the real workers.

(WSPU circular 1907)

'Intriguers whose device was to get hold of the Union' – this was how, with a complete lack of sisterly devotion, the Pethick Lawrence–Pankhurst clique in the WSPU described the dissidents who were to form the Women's Freedom League. What had caused the split and why were such leading suffragettes as Charlotte Despard, Edith How Martyn, Marion Holmes, Cicely Hamilton and Teresa Billington-Grieg subjected to such a bitter (and unfounded) attack?

In September 1907 Mrs Pankhurst had decided to select a new executive committee for the WSPU and to abandon its constitution and forthcoming conference. She was clearly worried that she was losing control as the organisation grew, and probably felt her position was threatened by other capable women such as Charlotte Despard and Teresa Billington-Grieg (Rosen 1974:89). Yet the rift was due to more fundamental political factors than a mere personality clash. First, democratic principles were involved and a basic disagreement over organisation. Christabel and Emmeline Pankhurst felt that militant tactics made an autocratic structure necessary; an army does not elect its generals. The women who left were increasingly sceptical about the wisdom of such an approach and could not swallow the contradiction of fighting for a democratic reform in an undemocratic organisation. Nor could they see how women would be able to develop their own autonomy if they were merely to obey orders from above. In the words of Teresa Billington-Grieg, later a critic of the whole suffrage movement (Billington-Grieg 1911), the Pankhursts may well have been geniuses or angels from heaven, but

still their claim would be evil and harmful to the cause, for it would rob the average woman of all opportunity of self government and self development . . . no angel from heaven was ever good enough, strong enough, or far-seeing enough, to be entitled to govern others . . . if we are fighting against the subjection of women to men, we cannot honestly submit to the subjection of women to women.

(2nd Annual Conference WSPU Report)

Secondly, the split reflected the growing conservatism of Christabel and her mother. By 1907 they wanted to appeal mainly to wealthy women, and the move to London in the previous year was a further break from their ILP and working class heritage. This break had been emphasised by the Pankhursts' insistence not to support the ILP candidate in a 1906 by-election at Cockermouth. To ILP members like Charlotte Despard and Teresa Billington-Grieg this new policy was a betrayal. All in all, the crisis of 1907 was not only caused by conflict over organisation and democratic principles but by a straightforward left and right split within the WSPU. In many ways, this was confirmed by the subsequent development of both organisations.

The 'seceding camp' decided to abandon its legitimate claim to the title WSPU and become the Women's Freedom League in November 1907 (*Women's Franchise* November 28, 1907). Its size is difficult to establish although it was probably the smallest of the three major suffragist bodies. David Rosen argues that only 20 per cent of the total WSPU membership left in 1907 (Rosen 1974:92) to join the League, but Teresa Billington-Grieg's estimates dispute this. She wrote that just over half of the original WSPU branches said they would attend the 2nd Conference in October 1907 (2nd Annual Conference WSPU Report), while by 1908 the League had 53 branches from Aberdeen to Clapham, Glasgow to Hackney (1908 Annual Report WFL). However, even the WFL itself claimed that it only had 4,000 members by 1914 (9th Annual Conference WFL Report) and the circulation of its paper, *The Vote*, was small, reaching a peak of over 13,000 for November 1913, but slumping to 400 weekly in 1919 (WFL Executive Committee Minutes December 14, 1912; July 15, 1919).

Unlike the WSPU, the Women's Freedom League did become a democratic organisation with annual conferences deciding policy and electing a national executive committee and a president. It claimed to be a militant society and, although it never adopted the tactics of the WSPU, there were 142 separate imprisonments of WFL members in 1908, and Alison Neilans became infamous for pouring acid into a Bermondsey ballot box in 1909 (Newsome 1957). It was the first suffragist organisation to hire a balloon to shower London with propaganda and it helped to organise both the Women's Tax Resistance League and the women's boycott of the 1911 census (*ibid.*). Militancy, it was made clear, was aimed solely at the Government, and the later methods of the WSPU were condemned. Indeed, after a bout of WSPU window smashing, one member claimed that had she been a shop-keeper faced with a stone-throwing suffragette she 'would have had a revolver and killed the first person' (WFL Special Conference Report 1912: 30). On the other hand, the early tactics of the 'baa lambs' of the NUWSS were seen as too soft and polite (Billington-Grieg 1909:8–9), but this criticism abated as the National Union developed a more aggressive policy.

Although the League had a democratic structure it is evident that some members, particularly Charlotte Despard, were more equal than others. In 1912 she was accused of autocracy, and several members of the Executive Committee resigned. Over one third of the delegates at a Special Conference in 1912 voted to remove her from the presidency. (WFL Special Conference Report 1912) and Teresa Billington-Grieg later accused her of becoming an idol (Billington-Grieg 1911:90–94). It is not difficult to see why she dominated the WFL and how her influence became a major component in its progressive image. Already in her sixties when the League was formed, Charlotte's grey hair covered by an old-fashioned mantilla and feet often shod in sandals gave her a striking appearance. Her relief work in the slums of Battersea led her into radical and socialist politics. She joined the Marxist Social and Democratic Federation in the 1890s, and the ILP in 1901. She became a pacifist during the War, a Labour candidate in 1918, and a supporter of Irish and Spanish Republicanism. When Charlotte Despard died in 1939, she was 95 years old; she was a truly remarkable woman (Link-later 1980).

Yet it was not only Charlotte Despard's influence that was to shape some of the more progressive political positions of the League. Other influential members, such as Teresa Billington-Grieg, also had radical and socialist backgrounds.

That the aims of the League went beyond the vote was made clear in *The Vote* and in its official programme. For example, *The Vote* claimed that 'its tone will be distinctly progressive. A paper that should remain neutral upon vital social questions could neither be very valuable nor interesting' (*Vote* September 8, 1909:1). The League's official object was not only 'to secure for Women the Parliamentary vote as it is or may be granted to men', but also 'to use the power thus obtained to establish equality of rights and opportunities between the sexes and to promote the social and industrial well being of the community' (*ibid.*). The apparent breadth of its demand was even reflected in its choice of title – the Women's Freedom League – as opposed to other proposals, such as the Women's Enfranchisement League, which were rejected (*Women's Franchise* November 14, 1907:227). What, then, were the feminist and political analyses of the WFL?

Although the League called for equal opportunities, one of its most striking features in its early days was the apparent acceptance of a woman's 'natural' domestic and maternal role. This was reflected in a series in *The Vote* called 'Suffragettes At Home'. Mrs Gill was shown dressmaking, Mrs Balham washing clothes, Mrs How Martyn making jam, Alison Neilans (of the Bermondsey Ballot Box incident) cleaning her stove, Mrs Hicks and her daughter spring cleaning, Mrs Agnes cooking and a 'Mrs Joseph McCaber' bathing her baby (*Vote* March–May 1910). All the stereotypes of women as housewives, childcarers and domestic workers were tacitly accepted, even welcomed, here.

Within the context of the pressures on women to pursue their 'natural' roles, this is perhaps understandable and may well have been influenced by tactical and strategical considerations. After all, it must again be emphasised that the very notion of women organising politically raised much opposition from men (and some women too) who felt it upset the 'natural order' of things. Nonetheless the call for greater opportunities outside the home alongside an apparent acceptance that home was where they really belonged, did present a contradiction. Even brave and fearless women such as Edith How Martyn, who had stood up to the Pankhursts and had been imprisoned several times, wrote: 'Many of us have a real liking for domestic duties – it is a great pleasure to hear one's family praising a new kind of cake . . . or one's handiwork in embroidery or other kinds of handicraft' (*ibid.* March 26, 1910:261).

These activities, although, of course, perfectly acceptable in themselves, were presented as specific female activities: the sexual stereotypes remained intact. A Mrs Shaw – who signed herself 'Mrs *Donald* Shaw' – further reflected this contradiction when she declared: 'No matter what profession or occupation a woman may take up, no matter how wide her scope may extend, she will always be a wife and mother first – by nature, by choice, by inclination. Women's sphere will always be the home [and] in producing and bringing up and training the children of the nation' (*ibid.* February 24, 1912:211).

As with the NUWSS however, the debate within the Women's Freedom League, even before 1910, began to broaden and other women were critical of what Cicely Hamilton called 'the Noah's Ark Principle' which declared that 'all human beings naturally and inevitably gravitate towards matrimony, pair off and beget children.' Writing in 1908, Cecily Hamilton, who a year later published a critical book on marriage, *Marriage As A Trade* (1909), added that the word 'woman' should not be synonymous with 'mother', and that motherhood itself should be but a part of women's lives (*Women's Franchise* January 2, 1908:311).

The debate within the League became increasingly provocative around 1909. The Women's Charter, for example, was warmly welcomed. In a detailed review of the Charter, which 'should find a place on every woman's bookshelf', *The Vote* responded favourably to its major proposals as well as to the analysis of 'woman the social serf' (*Vote* December 2, 1909:68). The League defended the Charter against those who felt it was a diversion from the struggle for the vote, for it was 'a striking summary of the chief disadvantages under which women labour' (*ibid.* April 9, 1910:287).

The WFL could be subtle, too, in its condemnation of the ways in which men saw women. In an attack on an exhibition of 'Fair Women' (invoking parallels with the Miss World protest of 1970), the League argued that it was

an insult to the sex as a whole. It casts a slight on those women – the drudges of the community – the mothers, the factory workers, the business women, the servants, the charwomen, who have lost their looks in doing the world's dirty work. It specialises in the silk clad and the careless, in whose who have trafficked in sex charm and it sets a wrong standard for men and women.

(*ibid.* May 7, 1910:13)

Fifty years or so before the 'Ms' campaign, one contributor to *The Vote* even asked, in an article entitled 'Sex War and Language', 'how much longer will women suffer themselves to live under the disability of having to put 'Mrs' or 'Miss' before their names, so that the world in general may know whether they are some man's property or still on sale, while men are always 'Mr'?' (*ibid.* February 18, 1911:207).

Humour was also used to make equally valid points – for example Maude Fitzherbert's brilliant satire on the Lords versus the Commons struggle (Fitzherbert 1910) – and the odd joke was just as telling: 'How's your wheat?' one farmer asks another. 'First rate.' 'Pigs doing well?' 'Fine.' 'That puny colt come around all right?' 'He sure did.' 'How's your wife?' (*ibid.* June 11, 1910:84). Cicely Hamilton even composed a new song for the women members of the Anti-Suffrage League. To the tune of 'Tramp, Tramp, Tramp' it went:

> Trot off home and mind the baby.
> Trot off home and mind the kid.
> This isn't Woman's sphere.
> You've got no business here.
> So Antis trot off home as you are bid.
>
> (*Women's Franchise* November 26, 1908)

Thus the WFL, besides poking fun at the 'antis', could outline some of the more subtle aspects of women's oppression. The League was also critically aware of the unequal position of women within marriage. In a popular pamphlet, *Some Economic Aspects of the Women's Suffrage Movement* (1909), the Reverend R.J. Campbell described wives as being 'absolutely at their husbands mercy . . . the husband is the wife's paymaster and she is immediately dependent on his bounty'. Moreover

in the majority of households the wife has to work as hard as the husband – probably harder, for her hours of labour are not fixed – but she has no recognised right to any standard wage as remuneration for her services, consequently the power of the husband over the wife is felt and realised by both all the time because of the material advantage placed in his hands.

(Campbell 1909:3)

The solution was 'one of the most necessary and urgent reforms of the future . . . the wife should be entitled to her own wage over and above the needs of the household to be expanded as she pleases' – that is, wages for housework (*ibid.*).

In identifying both housework as work and the economic power of men within the family, this surely amounted to another relevant and exciting contribution to feminist theory and the debate within suffragism. Yet the Reverend R.J. Campbell, whose pamphlet was based on a speech to the WFL in February 1909, left many theoretical and practical problems of his demand unresolved. How were wage scales to be determined and who was to pay? How would the vote enable the proposal to be enforced? More importantly, and in spite of his claim that not all women were suited to domestic work, there was no question of who would be responsible for housework. It left the sexual division of labour intact – it left women in the home.

Nonetheless, not all members of the WFL accepted their 'natural' role, and some argued again that suffragists were fighting for a choice for women. Furthermore, towards 1914, some evidence, although by no means overwhelming, of attempts to link women's sphere to their oppression can be found. Perhaps the most radical was Edith Moore's 'Women and Freedom' (*Vote* June 5, 1914). This was a four page article apparently based on some of the work of Edward Carpenter who had contributed to the WFL and knew Mrs Despard (*Women's Franchise* April 16, 1908:493; Rowbotham and Weeks 1977:118). Moore complained that 'no woman belongs to herself' and that men had forced women into the 'seclusion of the boudoir or the drudgery of the domestic hearth'. Quoting that 'forseeing and great thinker', Carpenter, she continued: 'What can any decently sensible woman think of her present position . . . what can she think of the lies under which she has to live – too numerous to be recorded; except all things are intolerable!' Moore went on to criticise the notion that women should be confined to motherhood and childcare, and she believed that women would never be free while 'woman is man's property'. Although vague as to how women's emancipation was to be won, Moore's article did suggest that it would need more than the vote.

Even so, Moore's argument co-existed with the more traditional claim that society was unbalanced because the unique qualities of women were unrepresented. In the month before Moore's article *The Vote* had published another article which stated that:

From the first dawn of history this difference in function . . . is brought to our notice. The hunter and the homemaker, the fighter and the peace centre . . . the masculine and feminine forces that work in the world's evolution . . . We are wanted on the world's councils because we are women and we have a woman's point of view.

(*Vote* May 8, 1914:42)

Suffragist feminism was nothing if not eclectic.

Throughout this period, of course, the Women's Freedom League was struggling for the vote. Although the WFL argued that this was part of a wider struggle (for example, *Vote* October 30, 1909:1), it certainly implied that the possession of the vote would have a funda-mental and qualitative effect on the lives of women. Indeed, Marion Holmes argued that the 'difference between the voter and the non-voter is the difference between bondage and freedom' (Holmes 1910). Like many of their sisters in the early years of the NUWSS, the members of the WFL believed that the possession of the vote would transform the lives of women: in particular it would increase the wages of women workers. 'If there is no connection, as our learned opponents in the House tell us,' *The Vote* declared, 'between the rate of wages and the possession of electoral power, we venture to think that it is a strange and terrible phenomenon that those who are unrepresented in Parliament are the worst paid members of the community' (*ibid*. August 20, 1910:195). Indeed, 'one of the strongest reasons for the immediate enfranchisement of Woman is that the vote will immediately alter their economic status' (*ibid*. April 22, 1911:305). Some voting men were paid badly, too, but this 'is not due to the uselessness of the tool he possesses, but to his own lack of skill in handling it' (*ibid*.).

All this implied that emancipation would come through reform and legislation. Perhaps Miss Hicks, who had featured in the 'Suffragettes At Home' series, summed up orthodox suffragist aspirations when she argued that she wanted the vote as a symbol of equality, and

as a means of bringing about that equality before the law; that the wife may be the equal partner of the husband and entitled to a fair return and to economic independence in return for her services in the home . . . that a woman may have the equal chance to undertake any work for which she is fitted and obtain the same rate of pay, for such work as a man if her work is as good as his.

(*Vote* March 19, 1910:248)

Gradually the political analysis of the Women's Freedom League widened and began to determine the relevance of economic power and class. This was partly due to the influence of leading members like Charlotte Despard, but was also connected with the industrial militancy of 1910–14. The League's support of the struggles of working women was another important factor; in particular, it was quick to condone their use of the strike. Sometimes this was explained in terms of being 'at present . . . their only way of focusing the public eye on their grievances' (*ibid.* April 22, 1911:305), but usually it went further. For example, *The Vote*, commenting on a strike and subsequent lockout of women workers in Sheffield, stated that 'we can only regard the recent frequency of these strikes and their uniform success as the outward and visible sign of the uprising of womanhood against industrial systems which attempt to take advantage of the handicaps of the female sex' (*ibid.* August 27, 1910:205).

The League constantly urged women workers to organise (*ibid.* June 25, 1910, for example), and argued that 'the évolution of the woman worker who realises her own importance in the general scheme of things is going to be a quicker process than the male capitalist is prepared to take. Every such realisation in whatsoever trade it is found helps us to bring nearer the day when cheap labour shall no longer mean female labour' (*ibid.* August 13, 1910:181). But the benefit of strike action went beyond showing that 'the value and the power of combination . . . is a great gain to the women workers, but it does not compare in value with the discovery that they have made of their solidarity . . . Women, conscious for the first time of the glory of their womanhood, are rising' (*ibid.* August 27, 1911:222).

These arguments implied that women's oppression, or its remedy, was not solely tied to the franchise but was connected with the wider economic and social system. This was further reflected in the League's language and the increasing use of the terms 'capitalist' and 'ruling class'. Yet the WFL did not become a socialist organisation, and old orthodox suffragist political analyses remained. For example, one article, '101 Points in Favour of Women's Suffrage', concluded that, for women workers, 'the only relief from their industrial burdens can come from their enfranchisement' (*ibid.* January 22, 1910:151). But the developing logic of the WFL's attitude was perhaps taking it beyond traditional suffragism. Certainly, the usual interpretation of the 'non-militants' of the NUWSS and the WFL needs urgent reappraisal.

Of course, the WFL's attitude towards working women did not come out of thin air. The links between the organisation and the Labour movement had always been strong and were, as has been described, indirectly responsible for the split from the WSPU in 1907. Charlotte Despard had a long association with the ILP as did other leading members such as Irene Miller and Teresa Billington-Grieg, who had become the ILP's first women's organiser in 1904 (A.J.R. (ed.), *The*

Suffrage Annual . . . 1913). Joint meetings with the ILP and other socialist organisations were not uncommon (*Vote* February 12; March 30, 1912) while, if the Middlesbrough branch of the WFL is anything to go by, there were rank and file links with socialist and Labour organisations. In response to a national enquiry, the branch replied to headquarters in London that, of its dozen or so members, two belonged to the ILP, one to the Women's Co-operative Guild and one to the Marxist British Socialist Party (Middlesbrough WFL Minutes). Unfortunately, only Middlesbrough's reply seems to have survived.

The WFL not only supported the struggles of working women in its paper, *The Vote*, but also became actively involved. For example, it worked among trade unionists and working women in Poplar in 1910, even before Sylvia Pankhurst organised her Federation in the East End (*Vote* January 15, 1910:135). By 1910, too, Charlotte Despard had formally and publicly asked the Labour Party for its full support in the battle for votes for women. 'My sympathy with your struggle,' the President of the WFL wrote, 'and my long years of work on behalf of the ideals of your Party make me earnestly hope that the claim of my sisters, for whom I speak, is at last, through you, to be fulfilled' (*ibid*. February 12, 1910:185).

Amy Sanderson, in a letter headed 'The Labour Party and Votes for Women', also appealed for its support although she was critical of its past attitude – 'a curious mixture of earnest championship, lukewarm support, indifference and hostility' (*ibid*. March 26, 1910:258). Nonetheless, she felt suffragists had a justified claim 'on a party that champions sweated workers, 82 per cent of whom are women'; and she also claimed that increasing numbers of liberal women, disgusted with the Liberal Government, 'are now turning a sympathetic ear to Labour (*ibid*.). Of course, this last sentiment had strategic implications, but the WFL's attitude towards Labour went beyond this. By 1912, at the Special Conference of the WFL, a motion calling on the League to 'identify itself' or 'strongly support' the Labour Party was discussed, and it was agreed that Labour candidates in three-cornered contests would be supported (WFL Special Conference Report 1912; 8th Annual Conference WFL Report 1913).

Yet not all members approved of the growing association of the WFL with the Labour Party, and at the 1912 Conference they not only accused Charlotte Despard of autocracy, but also of thrusting her own political views on to the League. It was revealed at the Conference that she had recently threatened to resign from the WFL and work full time for the Labour Party for 'she could not work with women' (WFL Special Conference Report 1912:26). Others felt that the League should have been struggling for all women, not just for those from the working class, or if they were to support Labour candidates, it should have been on strategic grounds only. Yet, although nothing akin to the NUWSS's Election Fighting Fund was set up (indeed, there was some friction between WFL and the National Union over this), Charlotte Despard stayed (WFL Special Conference Report 1912; 8th Annual Conference WFL Report 1913). Moreover, meetings with the ILP and even with the Marxist British Socialist Party not only continued after 1912, but seemed to increase (*Vote* June 8, 1912; November 7, 1913).

Allied to a growing class struggle this association further pushed the political analysis of the WFL to the left and indicated, crucially, that power did not solely rest with the possession of a parliamentary vote. In a review of the class conflict in late 1913, for example, Charlotte Despard argued that

those who have behind them the sinews of war – money and the physical force that money can command – are in the field. Fifty millions of hard cash with which the employers, backed by the Government, can soon obtain an obedient police force, magistrates and judges belonging to the order, prisons for active rebels and for the passive the sharp whip of hunger will speedily bring the struggle to an end.

(ibid. October 3, 1913:372)

The League made similar statements in its support of the militant class struggle in Dublin in 1913. Charlotte Despard, who became a fervent supporter of Irish Republicanism, argued, in praise of James Connolly and James Larkin, that 'we of the WFL . . . rejoice that the barriers of revolt against oppression and tyranny have been raised', and tried to link their struggles to her own (*ibid*. November 7, 1913:4). At a meeting attended by the ILP and the BSP, after Larkin's release in November another WFL member also declared the League's support for

he stands for the sweated worker – men and women – he stands for the little children whose crying want has been one of the assets on the Capitalists' side . . . 'We have been sacrificing our women on the altar of commercialism for a 1,000 years!' cried Larkin. So *we* have no difficulty in making our choice of sides.

(ibid. November 23, 1913:67)

Quite clearly the support given to the Labour movement went beyond a strategic relationship with the Labour Party. Charlotte Despard among others had called for a closer relationship between suffrage and Labour movements before the Party's vital decision of 1912 and, in any case, McDonald's support was hardly unequivocal (Morgan 1975:129). The result was a stretching to the limit of the political assumptions of suffragism. The emancipation of women was no longer a matter of the vote but tied to the liberation of a class. Not all members of the Women's Freedom League agreed with this and it did remain a suffragist organisation. Moreover, it could have appeared that the specific oppression of women would be lost to a general class struggle, although distinctions between the oppressions of working class men and women were made. For example, Charlotte Despard wrote in 1913 that 'property exists and property must be respected. Woman is man's inferior and must serve him. Propertyless man must labour, not on his own terms, but on the terms that property chooses to impose. If they refuse she is unsexed and he is a tyrant' (*Vote* October 2, 1913:373). A critique of the link between women's sphere and their oppression did not emerge, however, and the notion that 'truly women are the guardians of the home' (*ibid.* August 15, 1913:256) remained current.

All the same, the League could be very incisive on the results of the oppression of women and this was particularly clear in its attitude towards sex. Here, the attitude was the orthodox moral one that the only function of sex was for procreation, and the WFL, in common with the NUWSS, did not call for greater sexual freedom for women. However, the League was adamant on two points – first, that it was men, as a sex, who were responsible for the sexual oppression of women, and secondly, that the state's protection of women who had been abused was both hypocritical and inadequate. And the WFL did not pull any punches in the description of the horrors found in the London Lock Hospital for Women, described as the hospital for 'the victims of men and men's cruel lust' (*ibid.* June 27, 1913:147), or in its articles on prostitution.

The WFL's attitude was perhaps best reflected in a series, 'The Protected Sex', that appeared in *The Vote* in 1913 and 1914. This was originally launched, as the title implies, to counter the 'anti' claim that women were adequately protected by the law. It covered a multitude of recent court cases involving rape, incest and sexual assault. Besides attacking the behaviour of men, the League also showed how the law valued property far higher than women. One article in the series (October 17, 1913) reported that, for sexual assault on an 11-year-old girl, assault on a 4-year-old, and an assault by a father on his three daughters, the sentences were respectively six, two and three months. This was contrasted to the case of a mother with an unweaned infant who received six months' hard labour for receiving stolen goods. As the WFL argued:

It is upon your laws and lawgivers, our customs and conventions, in all matters in which sex is concerned . . . the talk about the purity of women is mostly cant. In marriages wives must be pure for the sake of the husband; in brothels a pure victim reaches higher prices; in the law courts chastity is a commodity of much lower value than property. Meanwhile men prate of purity.

(*The Vote*, August 15, 1913:256)

This feminist attack on men and the state was based on an acceptance that the ideal of monogamous morality was still an ideal worth fighting for. In the context of growing concern over the spread of venereal disease this is understandable, although some women were critical of such a position. There was little criticism in the WFL, however, save perhaps in Edith Moore's article on 'Women and Freedom' (*ibid*. June 5, 1914:104). Yet, as one member put it,

Is the debate over VD all our age has to contribute to the vaster world problem of sex relations? Are we incapable of approaching the greatest of human forces from any other aspect but that of the hospital and the police courts? Have we nothing but danger signals and taboos with which to guide the oncoming race?

(*ibid*. September 28, 1917:372)

A further fascinating insight into opinion within the WFL towards sex and reproduction was provided by the 9th Annual Conference. During a debate on a proposal from the League's Political and Militant Department it was suggested that 'a definite threat be made, embodied in letters to the PM, the Archbishop of Canterbury, and other authorities, that should Women's Suffrage be denied beyond a certain date, a campaign to assist working women to limit the birth rate be commenced' (9th Annual Conference WFL Report). The proposer of this startling idea, Mrs Huntsman, went on to say that upper and middle class women were already using birth control and that it would be easy to spread the information to their poorer sisters. This 'can be done with perfect ease . . . We have at least 20 members who are ready to do it, to go into the working class districts and tell their knowledge. It will spread itself' (*ibid*.). Although presented in a somewhat patronising tone, this was a radical idea, given the contemporary concern over the birth rate – an organised campaign along the lines suggested would not have been welcomed by the state. Other delegates also saw it as more than a mere tactic in the struggle for the vote, realising that it could give more women control over reproduction. For example, Eunice Murray recalled a pitiful case of a woman with 19 children who would have had only three if she had known how (*ibid*.).

But contraception was a tricky issue, and Eunice Murray seems to have been in a minority: the Middlesbrough delegate thought that the proposal would encourage immorality, and the Hampstead delegate felt 'that the only limitation that any decent women ought to indulge in is to lead a separate life' (*ibid*.). Charlotte Despard, still a devout Catholic, agreed. She felt that 'for us, the members of the WFL, for whatever cause, to teach artificial limitation of families would be wrong' (*ibid*.): it would make prostitutes of married women. 'What is artificial and wrong, and brought in merely for the wicked gratification of men and women, that is not fit we should speak of.' She did appear to be willing, privately, to talk of natural methods of control, but advised the Conference, 'do not bring among our sisters of the working class that which has been so evil for the women of other classes' (*ibid.*). The motion was defeated.

If the WFL had managed to launch such a campaign, it would unquestionably have aroused considerable opposition. The hypocrisy surrounding the Besant–Bradlaugh trial was far from dead, and concern over the size of the population would have created additional hostility. These restraints and the need to maintain respectability perhaps explain why the League rejected the idea. And an opportunity to launch a campaign of direct and immediate relevance to working women was lost.

The First World War came as a terrible shock to the Women's Freedom League; the only war it had envisaged in 1914 was a sex or class war (*Vote* June 19, 1914:142). Charlotte Despard's immediate appeal to her members, and all other suffragists, was to 'demonstrate everywhere . . . against our nation embarking on this criminal war' (*ibid.* August 7, 1914:262). On August 10th the League decided that at all costs it must 'keep the Suffrage flag flying' and this, in contrast to the WSPU and, to a lesser extent, the NUWSS, it did throughout the War. At the outbreak of the War it formed the Women's Suffrage National Aid Corps to help with the wartime distress of women and children (*ibid.* August 14, 1914:278).

The WFL's early explanations of the War were similar to those expressed by some members of the NUWSS: it was an inevitable result of a man-made world built on physical force, and showed dramatically, as the National Executive Committee put it, 'the supreme necessity of women having a voice on the counsels of the nation' (*ibid.*). Charlotte Despard also used this argument, but her opposition to the War ran deep, although, until her brother Field Marshal Sir John French was removed from his command in December 1915, she was guarded in her public comments. She was a member of the British section of the Women's International League, which had been founded by some of the women who had left after the split in the NUWSS; in 1916 she joined the No Conscription Fellowship (later the National Council for Civil Liberties); and, in February 1918, she left the presidency of the League to commit her energies to the Women's Peace Crusade (Linklater 1980:177–202). Although some members became wary of the League's association with Charlotte Despard's pacifism, this, together with its continued suffrage work, further enhanced the WFL's radical reputation.

Throughout the War the WFL was keen to protect and push the interests of women. Through the WSNAC it opened cheap cafes, made and distributed children's clothes and organised clinics and milk depots (*Vote* September 4, 1914). It even set up a toy shop in Hackney to provide employment for women (*ibid.* December 11, 1914:42). Along with Sylvia Pankhurst, the WFL was also instrumental in forming the League of Rights for Soldiers' and Sailors' Wives and Relations which pressed for better allowances and pensions. And it continued to struggle for the rights of women workers (particularly for equal pay) while fighting against compulsory War service (*ibid.* November 27, 1914:101; June 25, 1915:655). In this way the feminism of the League survived.

The League was most vitriolic in its condemnation of government attempts to reintroduce legislation akin to the Contagious Diseases Acts which allowed the compulsory medical examination of any woman suspected of passing venereal disease on to a member of the armed forces. With Sylvia Pankhurst's East London Federation of Suffragettes it campaigned against a possible introduction of regulation 40d of the Defence of the Realm Act (in reality, a Contagious Diseases Act) in late 1914, early 1915 and again in 1917 (*ibid.* December 4, 1914; January 18, 1915; September 28, 1917). Eventually 40d was re-introduced in 1918, and women found 'guilty' were liable to six months' hard labour. The WFL was aghast at such male hypocrisy and its implicit approval of prostitution. *The Vote*, continuing in the same vein as its 'Protected Sex' series, reported many cases where women were brought to court on the word of men. As Charlotte Despard argued: 'Damnable lying hypocrisy. The accused is sheltered, with none to contradict him, and the maligned victim has no redress. Can women be blamed for feeling that of all the cynical, one-sided laws that have ever been passed, this is the worst?' (Linklater 1980:187).

The advice to women workers to organise and unionise also continued, even in the middle of the War (*Vote* July 13, 1917:282), although the League's attitude to the sexual division of labour remained unclear. The Government's call for munition workers was seen as 'open acknowledgement that women's place is no longer in the home but in the nation' (*ibid.* March 26, 1915:541), whereas Charlotte Despard continued to claim that 'to women everywhere belongs the bearing and rearing of children. That is the work of myriads of women, that is their preoccupation' (*ibid.* December 22, 1916:52). A year later, she was still stressing that 'Bearing, rearing, training, loving the little ones . . . caring for the helpless, the sick, the defective . . . this is women's work, this is her interests' (*ibid.* February 2, 1917:100). Thus a clear analysis or denunciation of sex-bound characteristics or roles did not emerge, although, for example, Nina Boyle claimed that 'women's sphere is the world' (*ibid.* November 2, 1907:28).

The WFL welcomed even the limited measure of votes for women granted in 1918, although it would have preferred adult suffrage (*ibid.* February 9, 1917). It was adamant that its work was not finished and, in 1918, the WFL adopted a new wide-ranging programme that included equal pay, equal opportunities and demands for better housing and childcare (11th Annual Conference WFL Report). In the following year the League pressed also for increased trade unionism among women, a national minimum wage and government-run factories for newly unemployed women workers. The WFL remained independent from the political parties, although its warm relationship with the Labour movement continued and Charlotte Despard stood, unsuccessfully, for Labour in Battersea in December 1918 (*Vote* January 3, 1919).

The League, however, remained essentially a suffrage society, a fact in part responsible for its declining membership. And, in spite of its radical past, it could still support the political thinking behind orthodox suffragism. As Nina Boyle argued in January 1918:

We have the power to do more than just support men, we have won power to get and do the things that women choose to want. There is not a question so great that we may not dominate it if we choose . . . the vote is no useless, outworn weapon, and our victory, so long delayed, means power.

(*ibid.* January 25, 1918:124)

The importance of the Women's Freedom League to an understanding of suffragism is immense. When viewed in the context of the development of the NUWSS nationally after 1910, it appears that the 'non-militant' wing of the campaign for the vote associated itself increasingly with the Labour movement and the problems of working class women. Indeed, Beatrice Webb argued in 1914 that 'the whole of the women's movement finds itself side-slipping, almost unintentionally, into Labour and Socialist politics' (*New Statesman* February 14, 1914; see Pugh 1978:17). For many in the NUWSS and WFL it was more intentional than Webb implied, and for the League it went beyond mere strategic considerations. Together with the reactions to the militant struggles of the years from 1912 to 1914, the result for the WFL was a political analysis which argued that women's emancipation went beyond the mere gaining of the vote. This is the only logical conclusion that can be derived from some of the statements, especially Charlotte Despard's, made within the League, although the WFL never abandoned its demand for women's suffrage.

In the identification with working class women there was an inherent danger that women's oppression as a sex could be submerged and forgotten. However, the WFL's feminism included many aspects of the oppression women faced as women. The 'Protected Sex' series, for example, not only reflected the true values of the law but attacked the hypocrisy of men. It implied, too, that emancipation required change in the relationship between men and women. But the change, it seems, was not to be based on a new mode of sexual relationships, but on the ideals of the prevailing moral code. Similarly, there was little questioning of the sexual division of labour or of stereotyped sex roles: although some arguments within the WFL implicitly challenged the economic structure, the sexual structure was to remain the same.

Perhaps the WFL was in some ways restrained by its campaign for the vote. Certainly, more radical campaigns, as suggested at the 1912 Conference, would have hindered the struggle for the vote as would a more thorough-going analysis of women's sphere. Teresa Billington-Grieg may have summed this up in her resignation in 1911: she argued that the militancy of the WSPU and WFL had originally been designed to liberate women, and that the struggle for the vote was only one part of that process. She wrote of the two objects of militancy,

the smaller one was the early winning of the Parliamentary vote; the greater one was the woman's right to be herself, the undermining of the custom, habit and convention which bar the way to the real emancipation of women. [Now] the greater emancipation of women is being sacrificed in the haste for immediate enfranchisement.

(*Vote* January 21, 1911:159)

4 The Women's Social and Political Union

The woman has been sacrificed to the getting of the vote.
(Teresa Billington-Grieg, *The Militant Suffrage
Movement – Emancipation in a Hurry* 1911)

The WSPU was formed by a small group of women in Manchester in October 1903. Due to the militant tactics of the suffragettes – tactics ranging from window-smashing in London's fashionable streets to arson – it quickly became the most notorious (and most written about) suffrage society of the early twentieth century. Yet the emphasis on the Pankhursts' WSPU has until recently distorted our understanding of the suffrage movement. In particular it has disguised the other, equally valid, contributions of the NUWSS and WFL. Its militant tactics are generally assumed to reflect on equally 'militant feminism', although its ideas have not been fully explored. Certainly the suffragette campaign was in many ways unique, but it is just as inaccurate to assume its revolutionary nature as it is to regard the WSPU as the sole representative of English suffragism.

What, then, were its political and feminist ideas? The key to answering this question lies in a number of interrelating factors, perhaps the most important being, first, the WSPU's move away from its socialist and Labour background, and, secondly, the growing autocracy of Christabel and Emmeline Pankhurst. In the early days, the WSPU had a close relationship with working class and socialist organisations. All the Pankhursts were in the ILP, as were other founder members (S. Pankhurst 1931:168). Both Dr and Mrs Pankhurst had joined the ILP in 1894, and he had stood unsuccessfully for Parliament a year later (*ibid.*:119). Christabel had served her political apprenticeship with Eva Gore Booth and Esther Roper of the North of England Women's Suffrage Society which concentrated its activity among Northern working women (*ibid.*:164). The infant WSPU relied heavily on the ILP for support and organisation (*ibid.*) and it was also keen to attract working women like Annie Kenney and Hannah Mitchell (Kenney 1924; Mitchell 1968). Indeed, Mrs Pankhurst originally wanted to call the new group the Women's Labour Representation Committee and few could have seen the young WSPU as anything but an organisation for working class women.

All the same, Christabel Pankhurst was sceptical about Labour and socialist men's commitments to women's rights. She wrote in August 1903, in the *ILP News*, that socialists were silent on the position of women and, if not antagonistic, at least aloof: '– some day when they are in power, and have nothing better to do, they will give women votes as a finishing touch to their arrangements'; and she added, significantly, 'Why are women expected to have such confidence in the men of the Labour Party? Working men are as unjust to women as are those of other classes' (*ILP News* August 1903:42). The final break came in 1906 when Christabel 'intent on disengaging the WSPU from its connection with Labour' (Rosen 1974:70) insisted on an independent policy during the Cockermouth by-election. Previously the WSPU had worked for ILP candidates and (as has been described) this new policy was a bombshell to many ILP/WSPU members, some of whom left to form the Women's Freedom League.

The divorce from Labour circles was also connected with the reaction to the Free Trade Hall incident of 1905. This disruption of a Liberal meeting resulted in national publicity for the WSPU, and Christabel clearly felt that similar tactics would be more fruitful than working through Northern ILP circles. Behind this, too, was her growing desire to break the image of the WSPU as a class organisation; Christabel and her mother were already concerned over Sylvia's early work with women from the East End, and the WSPU's move to London in 1906 was partly designed to halt this. Christabel and her mother justified this development by arguing that the WSPU wanted to appeal to women of all classes, yet the implications were clear. According to Alice Milne, a working class member from Manchester on a visit to the new London Headquarters in 1906, 'if our Adult Suffrage Socialist friend could have looked in that room he would have said more than ever that ours was a movement for the middle and upper classes. What a fever our Union members in Manchester would have been in if such ladies made a decent [*sic*] on us' (Billington-Grieg papers).

Andrew Rosen argues that the breaking of the association with the Labour movement allowed the WSPU to grow to a point at which it no longer needed the ILP (1974:77): Christabel and Emmeline Pankhurst resigned from the Party in 1907. Yet the break also reflected a shift politically to the right. This was seen both in the split of 1907 and in the new election policy of the Union which stated that *all* Government candidates were to be opposed. In the politics of the 1900s this could only help the Tories, and, indeed, WSPU workers in elections were often dubbed 'Toryettes' (Fulford 1957:161). In fact there is some evidence that Christabel welcomed the possibility of a Tory victory in the January election of 1910 (Morgan 1975:64) and, by 1914, her intentions were clear: 'WANTED – A TORY GOVERNMENT. That a Tory Government may soon replace the so called Liberal Government is the keen desire of the WSPU' (*Suffragette* March 6, 1914:459).

Of course this could be seen as just another tactic in the attack on the Liberal Government, and it was often presented in this way, although there was little evidence to suggest that the Tories were any more likely to grant votes for women than was Asquith. Indeed, Teresa Billington-Grieg argued that the decision to oppose the Liberals without a firm pledge from the Tories was 'suicidal' (Billington-Grieg 1911:57). At the same time, this has to be seen in the context of Christabel's continuing antagonism towards the Labour Party, which she officially opposed in October 1912 (*Suffragette*, October 18, 1912:7). She had wanted the Parliamentary Labour Party to overlook mere 'questions of Trade Union finance' such as the crucial 1909 Osborne judgement which threatened to starve the party of funds; instead, Labour should 'force the hand of the Government by throwing their weight against them in every division with a view to driving them out of office' (*Votes for Women* February 16, 1912:308). For the Labour Party, hoping to squeeze through some of its programme with the help of the Liberal Government, this would have been political suicide; it refused. Thus, in Christabel's words: 'A Woman's war upon the Parliamentary Labour Party [became] inevitable' (*Suffragette* October 18, 1912:7). This position stood in marked contrast to that of the NUWSS and WFL, and reflected a fundamental difference within the suffrage movement.

Clearly, by 1910 many 'non-militants' were claiming that the vote, if not emancipation, was for working class women, and could only come through the activity of the latter. The WSPU leadership, on the other hand, claimed that their struggle was for all women but, as Mrs Pankhurst said, it was best fought for by 'the fortunate ones. At any rate, in our revolution it is the happy women, the women who have drawn prizes in the lucky bag of life . . . they are the women who are fighting this battle' (E. Pankhurst 1913:7). This essentially élitist attitude was evident as far back as 1906, and was emphasised both by militancy of the Union, and by the 1913 split with Sylvia Pankhurst.

In 1912 Sylvia had formed the East London Federation of Suffragettes among the working class women of the East End. Her insistence on running the ELFS on democratic lines and with working women rankled her sister: in Christabel's words, 'divided counsels inside the WSPU there cannot be' (Christabel to Sylvia November 27, 1913). What had particularly enraged Christabel, however, was Sylvia's appearance at a Herald League meeting with James Connolly and George Lansbury which had prompted the *Daily Herald* to remark that 'every day the Industrial and the Suffrage rebels march nearer together' (*Suffragette* November 14, 1913:95).

Christabel vehemently denied that 'the WSPU is marching nearer to any other movement or political party', especially the Herald League as it was 'a class organisation' (*ibid.*) and she reiterated that the vote would be won through all classes of women. Sylvia's account of the split, however, is more revealing:

> Their view of the difference . . . was that we had more faith in what could be done by stirring up working women . . . while they had most faith in what could be done for the vote by people of means and affluence . . . They said a deputation to the Labour Party was all very well for us, but one to the King was better for them.
>
> (ELFS Minutes January 27, 1914)

Only once, in the latter stages of the suffrage campaign and in stark contrast to the NUWSS and WFL, did the WSPU try specifically to organise working class women. This was in an attempt 'to prove once and for all that the demand for the franchise does not come from leisured prosperous women only' (*Suffragette* November 29, 1912:94). It was half-hearted and patronising, and fizzled out after the Reform Bill fiasco in January 1913 and the subsequent escalation of militancy. What could working women have thought of the advertisements in *Votes for Women* and *The Suffragette*? These implored readers to shop at the exclusive Derry & Toms (*Votes for Women* November 19, 1909), or to buy fur coats at a mere 195 guineas (*Suffragette* October 18, 1912:12) – on a rough calculation about eight years' earnings on a working woman's average wage.

Yet, if the history of the WSPU since 1906 shows a move away from its working class and Labour origins, it also reflects the growing autocracy of its leadership. Although Christabel later wrote that 'Mother and I were never the born autocrats we have been reported to be' (C. Pankhurst 1959:82), this was certainly not how it appeared at the time. As 'Christabel's Blotting Paper' put it, 'the true and inner secret of the Militant Movement was that we were an autocracy . . . the name of that autocrat was Christabel Pankhurst' (Kenney 1924:193). Indeed, the whole history of the WSPU is littered with breakaways by women who could not tolerate the dictatorship of the Pankhursts. The autocracy of Christabel and her mother was instrumental in the forma- tion of the WFL, and of *The Freewoman*, and in the departure of the Pethick-Lawrences in 1912, and of Sylvia Pankhurst in 1913.

An appreciation of the type of leadership pursued by the Pankhursts is crucial to an understanding of the WSPU. First, it is clear that many women could not participate in a struggle for a democratic right in a distinctly undemocratic organisation; and, secondly, an autocratic organisation is bound to reflect the opinions and policies – right or wrong – of the autocrats. 'Though active in a fight which demands the recognition of women as persons and individuals,' wrote Muriel Nelson, 'when the Voice speaks from Clements Inn [WSPU headquarters] we must voluntarily surrender our individual opinions, humbly fall in and follow' (*The Freewoman* December 7, 1911:51). How far could individual liberation be aided through working in an organisation that demanded unswerving acceptance of a policy decided by a self-chosen and unchallengeable élite? As Muriel Nelson implied and others found out to their cost, individual criticism was not allowed. Christabel may well have been a 'genius from heaven' (2nd Annual Conference WSPU Report: 4), yet it is by no means certain that her political strategy in the fight for the vote was always infallible. All the same, as far as Christabel was concerned, she alone knew how votes were to be won: it was merely 'a question of vision, the vision which is faith. We *see* that these methods are right and are ready to see them through to the end' (*Votes for Women* April 14, 1911:60).

It could however, be argued that militant tactics necessitated an élitist and conspiratorial organisation. It would have been foolish to discuss publicly daring (and illegal) actions that demanded secrecy if they were to succeed; as with any war, as the Pankhursts were fond of repeating, an army follows the direction of its generals. And by virtue of its very nature, a militant campaign had important feminist implications – the destruction of the stereotype image of woman as a frail and weak creature, incapable of physical force. Now women were to be found burning down empty houses, destroying racecourse stands and golf greens, cutting through telegraph wires, slashing valuable paintings and fighting with the police (S. Pankhurst 1931; *Suffragette* 1912–14). No wonder the Home Secretary, Reginald McKenna, horrified by the thousands of pounds' worth of damage caused, complained to the Commons that militancy was 'a phenomenon absolutely without precedent in our history' (Raeburn 1973:269).

The daring courage of the suffragettes involved was indeed remarkable, even though McKenna's knowledge of history and other struggles was not entirely accurate. Certainly, it is surprising that there were not more fatalities either as a result of force feeding or arising from battles with the police. Brailsford and Murray's *Treatment of the Women's Deputations by the Metropolitan Police* (1911) gives a clear picture of the brutalities suffered during one particular deputation to Parliament – on 'Black Friday', November 18, 1910. The suffragettes faced the growing hostility of many men, condemnation by the press as 'mad women' and 'criminals' (Rosen 1974:190), and the brutality of force feeding if they went on hunger strike. As the WSPU argued, force feeding could be regarded as torture, and many women suffered from its after effects. For example, the condition of one Scottish hunger striker, Miss Gordon, was described on her release as

appalling. Like a famine victim – the skin brown, her face bones standing out,

her eyes half shut – her voice a whisper, her hands quite cold, her pulse a thread
– her wrist joints stiff and painful – this was not from rough handling but from
poisoning. The breath was most offensive . . . and the contents of the bowel
over which she had no control, were appalling.

(Jones 1914)

Hunger strikers also had to face the Prisoners' Temporary Discharge
Act of 1912, better known as the Cat and Mouse Act. This allowed the
temporary discharge of hunger strikers until once more fit to serve their
sentence, at which time they were re-arrested: from April 1913 until the
outbreak of the War, Mrs Pankhurst was in and out of prison like a
yo-yo – imprisoned and released ten times (*Suffragette* April 1913–July
1914). If nothing else, suffragette militancy destroyed myths about the
physical capabilities of women.

   Admiration for the suffragettes' courage must not however cloud an
evaluation of the WSPU or of militancy itself. First, the militant
campaign, although causing thousands of pounds' worth of damage,
was only aimed at 'soft' targets – even at its most destructive during
1913 and 1914. Scarcely one important Liberal-owned factory suffered
attack, but empty houses and hayricks in Willesden were burned (*ibid.*
October 10, 1913:902). Hard economic targets were ignored, and the
WSPU's threat seemed insignificant when compared with the growing
militancy of Labour. Secondly, militancy in some ways became self-
defeating. Initially successful in gaining publicity, its own internal logic
demanded ever more daring acts which were met with ever increasing
hostility. Moreover, as Fulford points out, up until the Pethick-
Lawrences' departure in 1912, militancy was used as a political
weapon, coinciding, for example, with parliamentary debates, and
ceasing altogether, at one stage, in order to give the Conciliation Bill a
chance. After 1912 it became the servant of the leaders and linked more
to the imprisonments of Mrs Pankhurst. Although it kept the issue of
votes for women alive, its contribution to winning them must not be
exaggerated (Morgan 1975; Pugh 1978; and see chapter 7).

   Lastly, and most importantly, the militancy of the WSPU precluded
the involvement of most working class women, either individually or *en
masse*. Militant tactics tied to a wider social movement would, in fact,
have been far more effective. Certainly Asquith would no longer have
been able to treat the WSPU campaign simply as a 'law and order issue'
(Pugh 1978:18). In the words of Sylvia Pankhurst: 'Not by the secret
militancy of a few enthusiasts, but by the rousing of the masses, could
the gauge be taken up which not merely some Cabinet Ministers but
history itself had flung us' (S. Pankhurst 1931:416).

Even though the tactics of the WSPU distinguished it from the rest of
the suffrage movement it obviously shared the same aim – votes for

women – as well as some of the major feminist attitudes. It argued that
women's special interests were being ignored because they did not have
the vote (*Votes for Women*, October 1907:5), and that the political life of
the nation was subsequently unbalanced: when women voted,
Christabel argued, they would concentrate on 'the condition of the
children, the housing of the people . . . the care of the sick and aged
[and] the preservation of the home and family' (C. Pankhurst 1911).
And Emmeline Pethick-Lawrence added: 'For the sacred ideals of the
home, for the responsibility which we, as women, bear towards the
children and the future generations . . . we must take up arms and wage
this holy war of freedom' (*Votes for Women* June 11, 1908:334); when
women had the vote they would be even 'better comrades to their
husbands, better mothers to their children, and better housekeepers of
the home' (E. Pethick-Lawrence c.1908a).

Here, again, it is evident that the predominant roles of women were
accepted and used to justify the demand for the vote. This was particularly evident in the WSPU's reaction to the pressure on women to
rear a healthy and vigorous race. 'We women,' wrote Emmeline
Pethick-Lawrence, 'are often told that our most sacred duty and our
greatest privilege is the nurture and care of little children. We accept
that' (E. Pethick-Lawrence 1913:9). Previously she had claimed that
the whole struggle was to help women 'to rear a healthy race' (*Votes for
Women* August 5, 1913:9), and that 'it means the coming into the world
of new and noble race ideals' (*ibid.* January 1908:49). Part of a later
attack on the lust of men by Christabel was also couched in racial terms.
She denounced men's vice for degenerating the national stock and for
weakening the Empire through the production of half-caste children
(*Suffragette* May 8, 1914:86). Women needed the vote because they
knew they had 'a service to render, to the State as well as the home, to
the race as well as the family' (*Votes for Women* January 21, 1909:208).

While these arguments did not attempt to examine what was seen as
women's 'natural' role, the WSPU, like the other suffragist bodies,
made some telling observations on the inequality between men and
women. As Emmeline Pethick-Lawrence claimed: 'Women stand at
the very bottom of it all – however miserable the lot of the most
wretched and poverty-stricken man, there is always one being in the
world more miserably placed than himself, and that is the woman who
stands in nearest relationship to him' (*ibid.* June 25, 1908:344). Mrs
Pankhurst, too, accurately reflected the attitude of many men to
women when she wrote that 'some men think we are superhuman; they
put us on pedestals; they revere us; they think we are too kind and
delicate to come down into the hurly burly of life. Other men think we
are sub-human; they think we are a species unfortunately having to
exist for the perpetuation of the race' (E. Pankhurst 1914:12).

SUFFRAGETTE'S ADVENTURE IN AN AIRSHIP.

Miss Muriel Matters, as described on Page 5, attempted yesterday (accompanied by Mr. H. Spencer, the aeronaut) to reach the House of Commons in an airship. The picture shows the airship leaving Hendon. In the inset picture Miss Matters is leaning over the basket of the airship holding in her hands a megaphone.

The Daily Mail, *February 17 1909*

May Day in England 1913

THE SUFFRAGETTE FACE: NEW TYPE EVOLVED BY MILITANCY.

Mrs. "General" Drummond.

When attacking the police.

She is defiant.

Ecstasy on arrest.

Screaming with impotent rage.

Mrs. Pankhurst, the chief leader of the militant movement.

Youth looks like old age.

Dishevelled after fighting.

She uses supplication.

Rather emotional.

Addressing a crowd.

A male suffragist has to be protected from the crowd.

"Cads!" hisses a woman because the crowd jeered.

There is no longer any need for the militants to wear their colours or their badges. Fanaticism has set its seal upon their faces and left a peculiar expression which cannot be mistaken. Nowadays, indeed, any observant person can pick out a suffragette

resentful of anyone who is happy and contented and appear to be exceptionally bitter against the members of their own sex who do not support their policy of outrage. The public are becoming enraged at their tactics, and open hostility was shown to them at a

Typical press reaction to the suffragettes

The WSPU also shared some of the contradictions of mainstream suffragism. On the one hand, it called for greater opportunities for women, while, on the other, it accepted that their natural role lay in the domestic and maternal spheres. However, although this contradiction remained, some WSPU arguments did develop into an attack on the unequal power between men and women within marriage. For example, Christabel argued that women's right to work was one of the suffragettes' major demands, for 'the system under which a married woman must derive her livelihood from her husband – must eat out of his hand as it were – is a real great bulwark of sex subjection' (*Suffragette* January 16, 1914:310). Similarly, the real reason why the Civil Service, among other bodies, dismissed its women workers when they married was because of 'a desire to keep women in subjection. It is the desire to make of married women slaves [who] must depend for their protection and livelihood upon the good pleasure of another human being' (*ibid.* May 15, 1914:63).

Moreover, Christabel and others claimed that women's chores in the home were work and thus ought to be paid. Emmeline Pethick-Lawrence had already argued in 1911 that 'Neither the wage earning husband, nor the employer, nor the nation, has given due consideration to the economic value of this vast contribution of the married women's unpaid labour' (*Votes for Women* July 21, 1911:692). Christabel stated that housework had 'a money value. It is right, therefore, that a married woman shall get the same monetary payment for her work as is received for the work done by the rest of the community' (*Suffragette* January 16, 1914:310).

The arguments clearly had important implications for the feminism of the WSPU and for suffragist feminism generally. Certainly, it appears that the idea of wages for housework was not new and had the positive value then, as now, of identifying housework as work and its value to the economy generally. Yet in the case of the WSPU (and others) the specific details of how wages were to be quantified, and paid (and by whom) were omitted, and it was clear that housework was still considered the special reserve of women – again, the idea of the sexual division of labour remained. It should be added that it would be a gross mistake to view any of the suffrage organisations as strenuously pushing for this demand; it was but one idea of many that suffragism threw up. In the case of the WSPU especially, it was the vote that really mattered. As Christabel argued at the end of her discussion on women's work in the home: 'More important than anything else as a means of strengthening women's position, is, of course, the gain of the Parliamentary Vote. The vote is the symbol of freedom and equality' (*ibid.* January 16, 1914:310).

Indeed, it was the WSPU's attitudes towards the vote, and later

towards men, that distinguished it from the other suffrage organisations. Of course, as has been described, all of them wanted the vote for
various reasons, but to the WSPU it became almost an end in itself, and
the campaign a sacred, spiritual struggle. *The Suffragette* often alluded
to 'the sacred struggle . . . The women of the WSPU will pursue at all
costs this sacred object invoking the spirit of the Almighty in their
rightful struggle for civilisation. Our cry is "Votes for Women, Liberty
or Death!" ' (*ibid*. October 25, 1912:13).

Such language may have been understandable in the heat of the
militant campaign, but it also reflected the WSPU leaders' attitude
towards the vote. 'There is no department of life in which the possession of the Parliamentary Vote will not make things easier for women
today' (E. Pankhurst 1914:10): it would increase wages (F.W. Pethick-
Lawrence 1911), improve the law and prevent the sexual oppression of
women. It would, in short, end their subjection, for 'those who do not
trace the inferior position of women in all matters to their unenfranchised position look in vain for a reason' (*Votes for Women* March 4,
1910:351).

Implicit in these statements was an acceptance by the WSPU leaders
of the existing political system and its values. In particular, it rejected a
socialist analysis of power and the relevance of class. This was clearly
reflected (as has been described) in the development of the WSPU after
1906. It was not class, nor economic power that mattered, but *votes*.
Thus, as Mrs Pankhurst argued in a major WSPU pamphlet, *The
Importance of the Vote*: 'You get an 8 hour day for the miner but you get
nothing for women. Why? . . . because the miner has a vote. You see
what the vote will do. You see what political power will do' (E.
Pankhurst 1914:9). It was not trade unionism nor organisation that was
needed to remove low pay and poor conditions for women workers, but
the vote, for then 'the men employers and the working men will think
that, as women are citizens, they ought to have better treatment than
they have at the present time' (C. Pankhurst 1911). Indeed, Christabel
felt that strikes were really unnecessary and looked forward to the day
when they would be replaced by 'the political method, whereby the
elected representative of the employers, of the workers and of the
public at large discuss and arrive at a settlement' (*Votes for Women*
September 16, 1910:814).

It was a simplistic political analysis that revealed the ironic constitu-
tionalism of Christabel and her mother, as well as a conservatism that
was to be confirmed later, during the War. Their overbearing concentration on the vote also restricted debate – Lady McLaren's Women's
Charter, for example, was dismissed since 'the vote and nothing but the
vote is the only real charter for women today' (*ibid*. March 18,
1910:381).   Of course there were women within the WSPU who

disagreed with the leadership, but they either left or subdued their criticsm. In an autocratic organisation the views of the autocrats prevail.

The WSPU clearly regarded class division as unimportant and what increasingly mattered was the oppression of women – all women – by men. Thus new recruits were urged to leave any 'class feeling behind you when you come into the movement. For the Women who are in our ranks know no barriers of class distinction' (*ibid*. October 1907:6). By 1911, Emmeline Pethick-Lawrence even argued that the 'domination of the old ruling class has practically disappeared [but] the domination of sex remains in its age old form' (*ibid*. December 16, 1910:182). And, in 1912, during a year of increasingly militant class struggle, *Votes for Women* complained of the misuse of the term 'governing classes' by journalists as 'the governing classes today are the working classes, or rather the working men' (*ibid*. June 14, 1912:594).

As hostility to the militant campaign continued, the WSPU's emphasis on the oppression of all women as a sex increased. No doubt this was influenced by the brutality of the Government towards the suffragettes, but it led to a mistrust of all men and all male organisations. It possibly hastened the departure of Fred Pethick-Lawrence from the WSPU in October 1912, and it certainly led to a growing appeal to sex loyalty. Yet not all women agreed or could condone the attacks on the NUWSS for seeking 'male champions' of the Labour Party (*ibid*. July 19, 1912). Helena Swanwick, editor of *The Common Cause*, complained in 1911 that 'I would rather be loyal to my own conception of reason and right than to any theory of sex loyalty laid down by a self chosen architect' (Fulford 1957:246). Moreover, it ran counter to the attitudes of the rest of the suffrage movement – from the NUWSS to the WFL to Sylvia Pankhurst's East London Federation. These groups could also isolate and criticise male power over women but felt that class had to be considered too.

Perhaps the WSPU's hostility to men reached its zenith in 1913 with the publication of Christabel's curious *Great Scourge and How to End It*. This book, based on a series of articles in *The Suffragette*, now revealed the real reason for the opposition to votes for women – men's fear that women's suffrage would lead to a rigid code of sexual morality. 'All the high sounding arguments against giving votes for women are a sham – a mere attempt to cover up the real argument against this reform, which argument, we repeat, is sexual vice' (C. Pankhurst 1913:x). Men's immorality was so widespread that 75 to 80 per cent were consequently affected by venereal disease which they passed on to their innocent wives (*ibid*.:10). Thus 'out of every four men there is only one who can marry without risk to his bride. The cure for this horrific state of affairs? Votes for Women . . . and Chastity for Men' (*ibid*.:37).

Although Christabel's statistics were not backed by concrete evidence, fear of venereal disease was common and had led to the formation of a Royal Commission on the subject in 1913. Moreover, despite the wilder claims of *The Great Scourge*, it did indicate some of the causes of the sexual oppression of women. 'Sexual disease is due to the subjection of women. It is due to the doctrine that woman is sex and beyond that nothing . . . As a result of this belief the relation between Men and Women has entered on the physical' (*ibid*.:19–20).

Yet the 'Moral Crusade' that Christabel launched in 1913 was in many ways conservative, however shocking the lurid details of cases of venereal disease where 'the sex organs have to be removed by the surgeon's knife' (*ibid*.:42) or the vivid references to 'the secretion of the testicles . . . as the poisonous fangs of venomous reptiles' (*ibid*.: 61), may have been. It reflected Victorian attitudes to sex and the uncertainties about the sexual drive of men. Sex was sinful and its only legitimate purpose was procreation 'for the purpose of carrying on the race' (*ibid*.). If men found restraint difficult they should exercise self discipline and control, aided, if need be, by drugs. And, although Christabel's writing viciously exposed the reality of contemporary morality, it was based on its values which remained unquestioned: there was nothing on a woman's right to enjoy sex, nor anything on contraception.

Although the opposition to *The Great Scourge* and to suffragism in general was in part fuelled by male fears of a stricter morality, some radical feminists were also appalled by Christabel's tirade. Rebecca West, for example, argued that Christabel's remarks on sex were 'utterly valueless and were a matter for scalding tears' (D. Mitchell 1977:228), and Dora Marsden, editor of *The Freewoman*, was equally critical: if Christabel's figures on venereal disease were accurate then 'the number of those who are free from it neither means nor matters – we are all tainted and presumably inoculated in fact'; and she added, typically, 'If Miss Pankhurst desires to exploit human boredom and the ravages of dirt she will require to call in the aid of a more subtle intelligence than she appears to possess' (*ibid*.: 229).

The Great Scourge, and the 'Moral Crusade' of which it was a part, perhaps reflected the political bankruptcy of Christabel Pankhurst and the militant campaign. But her attacks on male attitudes and behaviour, and on the intransigence of Asquith's Government were understandable, although neither sex nor politics were as black and white as she argued. David Mitchell even proposes that a major reason for the launching of the Crusade was to revive a flagging WSPU, desperate for more notoriety and publicity, and, on this level, it worked (*ibid*.:229–230). The attitudes in *The Great Scourge and How to End It* were not new, nor revolutionary, however shocking some of the details. And, in spite of the contemporary restrictions on a free discussion on sex, they certainly were not militant.

The First World War finally exposed the basis of the political philosophy of Christabel and Emmeline Pankhurst. According to Sylvia Pankhurst, 'the WSPU entirely departed from the Women's Suffrage Movement. Giving its energies wholly to the prosecution of the War, it rushed to a furious extreme, its Chauvinism unexampled against all Women's Societies' (S. Pankhurst, 1931:593). The Union became rabidly nationalistic and xenophobic – its patriotism and anti-pacifism were unparalleled. The interests of women were submerged beneath the interests (or rather, what Christabel Pankhurst thought were the interests) of the nation. *The Suffragette* became *The Britannia* in October 1915, and was briefly suppressed in the latter part of the year and the early months of 1916, not for any reason to do with a women's struggle, but wholly as a result of Christabel's exaggerated and wild accusations about traitors within the Government. The War ended with Christabel standing as 'Patriotic Candidate and Supporter of the Prime Minister and the Coalition' at Smethwick, calling for 'British for the British' and a campaign against the rising menace of socialism. Her mother stood for the Tories at Whitechapel 10 years later.

Yet the WSPU's initial reaction to the War was in line with other suffragist thinking – war was due to the follies of a male world built on the male characteristic of physical force: 'This then is the world as men have made it, life as men have ordered it. A man made civilisation, hideous and cruel enough in time of peace, is to be destroyed . . . This great war . . . is Nature's vengeance, is God's vengeance upon the people who held Women in subjection' (*Suffragette* August 7, 1914:301). Significantly, feminine France had to be saved from the male Hun.

But the patriotism of the WSPU leadership quickly overwhelmed this traditional suffragist analysis. 'Second to none in Patriotism', *The Suffragette* declared as it began its chauvinistic support of the War (*Suffragette* August 14, 1914); and Joan of Arc ceased to be 'A Famous Militant' and became instead 'The Great Patriot' (*ibid*. May 16, 1913; May 14, 1915). The Union was the first to hand out white feathers to those men who did not enlist, and among the first to call for national conscription for men and women (*ibid*. June 11, 1915:136). It saw the evil work of the Germans everywhere, be it in industry (where they organised strikes) or in government where they sabotaged the war effort (*ibid*. July 23, 1915:227; *Britannia* March 10, 1916:145).

Lloyd George, once 'crooked and discreditable' (*Votes for Women* November 10, 1911:88), now ironically became the WSPU's new hero, and he was quick to harness their patriotic fervour to recruit women workers and, later, to counter industrial unrest. Thus with Government help the WSPU arranged a 'Women's Procession' in July 1915 organised as a 'Women's Right to Serve' demonstration. One of its major aims was to help Lloyd George to overcome trade union resistance to dilution and the employment of women (Mitchell 1977:258). The WSPU cared little for the fears of the unions and Mrs Pankhurst accepted the Government's feeble commitment to equal pay for women workers, as outlined by Lloyd George in his speech to the processionists. When, in response to his call for a fight for freedom, he was heckled by two women – 'we have not our freedom . . . will you give her a vote Mr Lloyd George?' – his reply – 'We will get her into a shell factory first' – went uncriticised by Mrs Pankhurst (*Suffragette* July 23, 1915).

Indeed, the vote, for which suffragettes had died and suffered imprisonment, now seemed of secondary importance to the WSPU. The same Christabel Pankhurst, the self-styled champion of women's rights who had denounced the horrific oppression of women by disease-ridden men, now argued that in 'English speaking countries . . . Women's liberty is greater . . . Women's position is higher . . . Women's influence and political rights were more extended than in any other part of the world' (C. Pankhurst 1914:6). Women who had previously heckled Christabel with demands for the vote were ignored (*Daily Sketch* August 16, 1914), while Asquith's conversion to women's suffrage was condemned because the WSPU feared it might take precedence over the claims of unenfranchised military men. In what amounted to an acceptance of the old 'physical force' argument of the 'antis', *The Britannia* declared that should the soldiers and sailors not be given the vote, then 'the flower of British manhood will be disenfranchised and the worst and weakest men will in consequence possess more of a voting strength than before' (*Britannia* August 18, 1916).

During the War, the élitist, racist and conservative thinking of the WSPU leadership became crystal clear. The traditional authoritarianism was reflected in the splintering away of two groups, the Suffragettes of the WSPU and the Independent WSPU, who were critical of the Pankhurst line on the War and on women's suffrage. Christabel, her mother and Flora Drummond were rabidly anti-German. Though silent on the German heritage of the Royal family (who conveniently dropped 'Saxe-Coburg' and became 'Windsor' in 1917), the WSPU, or what remained of it, demanded that all official organisations should be 'purified' of naturalised Germans and those born in England of German blood. By 1916, all aliens, *The Britannia* urged, should be interned (*Suffragette* July 9, 1915:198; *Britannia* July 7, 1916). Anti-German feeling in 1916 was not unusual – but the extremes to which the WSPU took it was. Any talk of peace by 'cranks' such as the Union for Democratic Control (told to 'go to Germany' by Christabel), or any attempt to democratise the War effort, was disloyal and deserved imprisonment (*Suffragette* May 14, 1915:75; August 27, 1915:288). No compromise with Germany was possible; all pacifists, like their old friend and supporter, Keir Hardie, were traitors. Hardie, an old supporter of votes for women, was in fact portrayed in a cartoon receiving the Nobel Peace prize from the Kaiser – 'Also the Nobel Prize (tho Tardy), I now confer on Keir Von Hardie' (*ibid.* July 30, 1915).

Christabel and Emmeline Pankhurst's attitude towards pacifism (seen as a left-wing cause) was related to their attitude towards socialism and class in the War: it was the 'national interest' that mattered, the fight between the Empire and the Hun. Not class nor sex differences, but nationality mattered now. The Pankhurst advice, according to Annie Kenney, was to 'forget our own internal family differences' (*ibid.* May 28, 1915:107) and concentrate on the battle against Germany. For Christabel, 'that old delusion, class war, is exploded. The interests of the Nation are one and indivisible. The true, the natural and the divinely intended human grouping is according to nations' (*ibid.* September 17, 1915:325). Thus women, such as Sylvia Pankhurst and Emmeline Pethick-Lawrence, who attended the International Congress for Peace at the Hague in 1915, were attacked since 'The Women of the Enemy Country Are Our Enemies' (*ibid.* April 16, 1915:4; April 23, 1915:25). So much for Christabel's sororial consciousness.

The antipathy towards socialism and Labour continued as the War dragged on. The WSPU, backed to the tune of £15,000 by leading capitalists (D. Mitchell 1977:265), launched an 'Industrial Campaign' in 1917 against the rising tide of industrial militancy, opposition to the War and 'Bolshevikism' (*Britannia* April 9, 1917). These blights were not seen as evidence of a growing revolutionary struggle against the War and capitalism, but were considered the work of the dark and mysterious 'Unseen Hand' driven by Bolsheviks and Germans (*ibid.*). 'Bolshevikism', after Asquith, Men and Germany, was the new Anti-Christ to be fought – or, as *The Britannia* called it, the 'new Anti-Suffragism' (*Britannia* February 1, 1918). Thus Christabel demanded the burning of socialist books by 'the public hangman' (*ibid.* August 30, 1918:107); warned Britain of the disciples of 'Mr Trotzsky' (*ibid.* February 1, 1918); claimed, in another shot in a hostile campaign dating back some 12 years or so, that the Labour Party was 'riddled with Bolshevikism and more and more dominated by the Bolshevist leadership of the MacDonalds' (*ibid.*); and argued that, after all, had not 'Bolshevikism' been invented by a German, Karl Marx? (*ibid.* March 22, 1918) – hardly a simplistic argument. The feminism of the WSPU did not entirely disappear during the War. Nevertheless, when soldiers' and sailors' wives were being spied on – to check that they were not infringing their rights to separation allowances – when food prices rocketed, and when the Defence of the Realm Act made legal the compulsory medical examination of women suspected of prostitution, the Union made little or no objection. Brief but half-hearted noises about equal pay were heard; and Flora Drummond summed up official policy when she declared on the Clyde that, although she favoured equal pay, 'just now I am less concerned with what they earn than that they are helping their country' (*ibid*. March 31, 1916:158). The great lack of relief work stood in marked contrast to the activity of the WFL and NUWSS. The WSPU's only practical help for women seems to have been the War Babies scheme to care for illegitimate children (*ibid*. May 7, 1915). It was not a success, and is perhaps mainly interesting, given the tirades of *The Great Scourge*, in its assistance to the results of immorality. Presumably men's immorality in wartime was excusable.

In November 1917 the WSPU became the Women's Party, with Mrs Pankhurst as treasurer, the ever faithful Annie Kenney as secretary, Flora 'General' Drummond as chief organiser, and Christabel as editor of *The Britannia*. Not surprisingly it was immediately denounced by the other suffrage societies who wanted to disassociate themselves from Pankhurstian extremism and who realised that it 'will of course be an autocracy like the old WSPU (*Cause* November 9, 1917:361). Nonetheless, the Women's Party manifesto did contain some interesting proposals: it called for equal pay and opportunity, a demand for better pre-natal care, for creches, even for co-operative housekeeping. There were demands, too, for equal parental rights and marriage laws.

However, there was no specific strategy for fulfilling these aims, and they must also be considered within the context of the whole programme of the Women's Party. Again, the extreme conservatism of Christabel Pankhurst becomes clear: workers' control was condemned as a German plot, and industry, Christabel explained in *The Britannia*, was to be left to its captains, for example, Lord Leverhulme (*Britannia* December 7, 1917:209). Indeed, the Women's Party manifesto declared that

All action on the industrial front is to be based on the principle that the interest of the community as a whole transcends that of the employer on the one hand and the employed on the other and that Parliament, as the sole representative of the Nation, must have the last word in all questions affecting the relations between Capital and Labour.

(*Women's Party Programme* 1917:4)

Class conflict and economic power were again ignored; equality would come through the vote. The workers were to be led and become mere cogs in the machine – or, as Christabel once remarked, 'let them be workers during working hours and ordinary human beings the rest of the time' (*Britannia* December 7, 1917). The appeal to patriotism, the denial of class conflict, the racism and virulent anti-socialism were almost fascist, and it is not surprising that members like Drummond later joined the extreme right wing Empire League, and Mrs Dacre Fox and Mary Richardson, Mosley's British Union of Fascists (D. Mitchell 1977:277). The Women's Party, which stressed that it 'is no way based on sex antagonism' (*Women's Party Programme* 1917:1), had little to offer a working class decimated and ravaged by war, and even less to offer women. It was a sad but logical end to Christabel and Emmeline Pankhurst's direction of the WSPU.

The traditional image of the suffragettes clearly needs revision, yet it would be inaccurate to dismiss totally the WSPU because of the ever increasing reactionary and limited views of its leaders. Their militancy alone was important in destroying some of the contemporary notions of the capabilities of women. More local studies of the organisation are required even though the Union was deliberately centred on London in the early years of the campaign. Further, it is difficult to accept, however politically misguided the militant campaign may have been in terms of obtaining votes for women (Pugh 1978:18), that suffragettes were willing to risk their lives purely for the vote or in misplaced heroine worship of the Pankhursts. Many of the feminist arguments within the WSPU, whatever their limitations, need careful evaluation to further an understanding of suffragist feminism. The attitudes towards housework and the analysis of men's ideas on women are particularly revealing, even though the former confirmed the domestic role. However, although the WSPU could isolate some elements of the specific oppression of women, it refused to question class differences or to see emancipation other than in terms of gaining the vote.

But perhaps the final criticism of the WSPU should be left to a contemporary and founder member, Teresa Billington-Grieg. A Manchester teacher and ILP member, she became disillusioned with the suffrage movement, although instrumental in the formation of both the Union and the WFL, and left it in 1910 to concentrate on writing. In 1911 she published *The Militant Suffrage Movement – Emancipation in a Hurry*. In this book she describes herself as 'a feminist, a rebel and a suffragist' who wanted emancipation from 'all shackles of law and custom, from all chains of sentiment and superstition' (Billington-Grieg 1911:1–2). Her view was that votes were important, but that they were not a 'panacea for all evils', and liberation would certainly not come 'through emotionalism, personal tyranny and fanaticism' (*ibid.*:3) – a clear reference to the WSPU. Indeed, Teresa Billington-Grieg's book was severely critical of the WSPU – on political, feminist and tactical grounds. In particular, she felt militancy was a sham, 'not real . . . dangerously and determinedly conventional', whose purpose rapidly became merely one of advertisement (*ibid.*:4). She condemned, too, the WSPU's break with its socialist origins and its courting of wealthy women.

Gradually the movement has lost status as a serious rebellion and become a mere emotional obsession, a conventional campaign for a limited measure of legislation, with militancy as its instrument of publicity and the expression of its hurry. The leaders of the militant movement do not want a revolution; we were mistaken who believed that they did; they would be afraid of one.

(*ibid.*:113)

Teresa Billington-Grieg was also convinced that militancy within an autocracy prevented independent thought and limited feminist debate. She was especially virulent in her attack of the orthodox argument that women should enter politics, in order to bring into it the ideals of the home. To her this was a

proof of the crude and limited rebellion that has been kindled by suffragette methods . . . The suffragette who is content with the home as it is, built on the subjection of the woman . . . is not a true rebel . . . Any woman who is really a rebel longs to destroy the conventions which bind her in the home as much as those that bind her in the State.

(*ibid.*:159–160)

And, finally, Teresa Billington-Grieg made a telling criticism when she complained of those many suffragists who 'fail to see that large areas in which emancipation is needed lie entirely outside the scope of the vote' (*ibid.*:173).

A 'famous militant' conscripted to patriotism

Dora Marsden, editor of The Freewoman

5 'A Nauseous Publication': *The Freewoman.* November 1911–October 1912

. . . the dark and dangerous side of the 'Woman Movement'
(Mrs Humphrey Ward quoted in *The New Freewoman* August 15, 1913)

The Freewoman was published as a 'weekly feminist review' between November 1911 and May 1912. In May 1912 it described itself as a 'humanist' paper, and by the following October, due to lack of finance, it collapsed, briefly resurfacing as *The New Freewoman: An Individualist Review* in 1913. The readership of *The Freewoman* was probably small, if only because of its high price of 3d, although no circulation figures are available. One surviving subscription list reveals over 300 subscribers, many of them suffragists, but the total number of readers clearly exceeded this. Although *The Freewoman* in its original form barely lasted a year, its importance to a fuller understanding of both suffragism and feminism is immense. It shows, in particular, a developing contemporary awareness among women involved in the struggle for the vote of the feminist and political limitations of orthodox suffragism.

The paper was established by Dora Marsden and Mary Gawthorpe, and backed by the radical publishers, Jonathan Swift. Both women had been in the WSPU, and Mary Gawthorpe had been an enthusiastic member of the ILP in Leeds (Gawthorpe 1962; S. Pankhurst 1911:98). She had been particularly active in the suffragette movement. She was arrested in the first WSPU rush on the House of Commons in 1906 (*Freewoman* August 1, 1912:215) and had written *Votes for Men* for the Union in 1908. She resigned from the WSPU in 1911, partly because of ill health but also because of its continuing autocracy.

However, it was Dora Marsden who was the real inspiration behind the paper. Described by Emmeline Pethick-Lawrence as a 'dear beautiful spirit . . . the sweetest, greatest and bravest of suffragettes' (E. Pethick-Lawrence to Dora Marsden October 6, 1909), and, by Sylvia Pankhurst, as having 'a face like a Florentine Angel' (S. Pankhurst 1911:367), Dora Marsden had also been an energetic WSPU member. She originally joined in Manchester, where she was arrested several times, once for heckling Churchill from a glass roof – only a policeman catching her ankle saved her from falling to an early death (*ibid.*:463). In 1909 she became the WSPU's organiser in Southport, but her independence and disorganised accounting led to her resignation in January 1911 (Marsden to E. Pankhurst January 27, 1911).

It was after her resignation that Dora Marsden, backed by her friend Mary Gawthorpe, decided that a revolutionary feminist paper was needed. Mary, later to become co-editor, urged Dora to try and enlist the support of Fabian women (Gawthorpe to Marsden May 25, 1911), and subsequently of the Women's Freedom League (Marsden notes; Dyson papers). Partly because of Dora's insistence on editorial independence, her relationship with the WFL came to nothing. But finally Charles Granville of Swift's came to the rescue, and was to back the paper until October 1912. Mary resigned in March 1912 to be replaced by Rona Robinson and Grace Jardine.

Under Dora Marsden, *The Freewoman* became a radical and free-thinking paper, open to the talents and ideas of Rebecca West, H.G. Wells, Edward Carpenter, Havelock Ellis, Teresa Billington-Grieg, Ada Nield Chew, the anarchists Guy Aldred and Rose Witcop, Stella Browne, and many others. Harriet Weaver, a life-long friend of Dora Marsden, claimed that the paper 'must have been edited on a mountain top, it breathed so heavily of freedom' (Lidderdale and Nicholson 1970:53–4), and Carpenter wrote, on its demise, that it had been 'so broad minded and courageous, that its cessation has been a real loss to the cause of free and rational discussion of human problems' (*New Freewoman* August 15, 1913:100). The paper itself, never known to show false modesty, claimed in its first issue that

> its publication marks an epoch. It marks the point at which feminism in England ceases to be impulsive and unaware of its own features, and becomes definitely self conscious and introspective. For the first time, Feminists themselves make the attempt to reflect the Feminist movement in the mirror of thought.
>
> (*Freewoman* November 23, 1911:3)

'Mirroring thought' is perhaps the best way to describe *The Freewoman* for it did not have a programme but acted as a forum for a radical and revolutionary discussion of women and politics. The discussions of women's sphere, marriage, sexuality and reproduction were all the more outstanding for their explicit criticism of contemporary moral codes and values. As Mrs Humphrey Ward, a leading anti-suffragist, implied, the ideas of *The Freewoman* represented a more revolutionary aspect of the women's movement (see Appendix II); perhaps it was this fear, rather than the prospect of women voters, that really motivated the opposition to suffragism.

The initial emphasis in *The Freewoman* was critical of suffragism, but from a radical and feminist perspective. Indeed, the paper argued that 'feminism is the whole issue, political enfranchisement a branch issue and the methods, militant or otherwise, are merely accidentals' (*Freewoman* November 23, 1911:3). Suffragist arguments reflected 'an unthought out and nebulous feminism', partly because free discussion within their ranks was 'systematically discouraged' (*ibid.*). Suffragism was also criticised for over-valuing the usefulness of the vote and thus misdirecting women's efforts. The women's suffrage movement had 'for years used up women's energies and diverted them from channels which could ill be spared' (*Freewoman* December 14, 1911:64).

Many contributors questioned suffragist faith in the vote. For example, H. Jackson argued that votes for women was an absurd aspiration but necessary – 'absurd because women have awakened to a desire for the franchise at a moment when the franchise has almost become a discredited thing . . . necessary because the illusion of the invincibility of the vote is still one of the most persistent beliefs of civilization' (*ibid.* December 28, 1911:104). 'G.E.M.' similarly criticised 'the average suffragist who refuses to think beyond that blessed day when "le Roy le veult" is subscribed to a Suffrage Bill extending the franchise to women' (*ibid.* January 18, 1912:172).

Much of the criticism in *The Freewoman* was specifically directed at the WSPU. Echoing Teresa Billington-Grieg's observations, militancy was attacked as a narrow policy that prevented genuinely radical thinking within the WSPU: 'Militancy takes the place of thought . . . militancy is the astutest possible move to keep thought quiet' (*ibid.* July 11, 1912:143). Guy Aldred, a regular contributor to the paper, was particularly critical of the aims of the WSPU leaders. He argued that 'it is not what we do, but what we aim at doing, what we yearn for and what we are . . . The trouble with militant tactics is that they lack a militant aim' (*ibid.* January 8, 1912:179). And he added later that 'to struggle by unconventional means for conventional privileges, when so many of the privileges mean nothing real, nothing of value to mankind, is rather to betray than enhance the cause of women's emancipation' (*ibid.* February 8, 1912:236).

The 'trinitarian dictatorship' (Billington-Grieg, *Freewoman* December 14, 1911:70) of the WSPU came under particular fire with Christabel, the 'voice of Clement's Inn', described as a leader of 'bondswomen' (*Freewoman* December 7, 1911:51). The WSPU leadership was even accused of 'purposefully avoiding victory' after the resumption of militancy in 1912, in order to maintain their self-importance and prestige. Bruce Glasier remarked as early as 1904 that 'the pair [Christabel and Emmeline Pankhurst] are not seeking democratic freedom but self-importance' (D. Mitchell 1977:51), and *The Freewoman* strongly echoed his sentiments.

Bit by bit it became clear why they had thwarted all efforts towards combination with other suffrage societies, why the working classes would have nothing to do with them . . . the paramount interest of the WSPU was neither the emancipation of women nor the vote, but the increase of power of their own organisation, absolutely limited in authority to three leaders and one male outsider.

(*Freewoman* March 17, 1912:304)

Not surprisingly, the attacks on the WSPU brought considerable criticism from suffragettes. Mary Gawthorpe in particular was unhappy with Dora Marsden's early broadsides and had to suffer accusations of being a traitor to the WSPU and of resorting to character assassination (*ibid*. December 7, 1911:44; Gawthorpe to Marsden March 22; 24, 1912). Yet, as Teresa Billington-Grieg asked, 'how [can] a personal dictatorship be adequately criticised without introducing personalities?' (*Freewoman* December 14, 1911:70). Nonetheless, some of the criticism of the WSPU was extremely harsh and perhaps Mrs I. D. Pearce gave a more balanced evaluation when she wrote that, whatever the extent of Christabel's egoism, the suffragettes 'have helped to arouse and awaken the people to a new interest in our question and have stimulated the great mass of the law-abiding supporters of it to such new life and energy that they can no longer be disregarded by those in authority' (*ibid*. December 28, 1911:112).

The debate within the paper seems to have been less critical of the NUWSS and the WFL, although Charlotte Despard's growing autocracy was also attacked (*ibid*. July 11, 1912:143). The task of both the Union and the League was 'to find momentum in the thought, the philosophy, the tendency, which suffragism represents' (*ibid*.). Yet they, too, had few ideas. In a long attack on suffragism, the paper claimed that there 'is no idea behind English suffragism . . . no feminism', and that its leaders stood ultimately to 'defend the Capitalist monopoly [and] the marriage monopoly'; and it concluded that 'all things considered suffragists are safer without a programme. To want a vote, and want it now, is a small affair, but it has the merit of sincerity' (*Freewoman* July 4, 1912:123; and see Appendix II).

In spite of this critical stance, it appears that *The Freewoman* was well known to suffragists and was read by many of them (it is impossible to judge exactly how many). Dora Marsden claimed that 'it is read by some suffragists in every large suffrage society in England' (*ibid*. July 11, 1912:142). All three suffragist journals, *The Common Cause, The Vote* and *Votes for Women* had advertised the paper, although they probably regretted it later. For example, Millicent Fawcett only read one copy and 'thought it objectional and mischievous and tore it up into small pieces' (Strachey 1931:235); and her fellow member on the Executive Committee of the NUWSS, Agnes Maude Royden, called it 'nauseous' (*Freewoman* July 11, 1912:142). But other suffragists disagreed. Ada Nield Chew, for example, welcomed it as 'meat and drink to the sincere student who is out to learn the truth, however unpalatable the truth may be' (*ibid*. April 18, 1912:435). Another, Robena Nicholson, President of the North Middlesex Women's Suffrage Society, wrote that such 'a paper was badly needed . . . I feel so keenly that we must do all we can to further any Feminist movement in England' (*ibid*. November 30, 1911:30).

The discussion in *The Freewoman* contrasted sharply with that within the major suffragist newpapers. Writers in this 'objectionable' and 'nauseous' journal were also interested in knowing how women as a sex came to be oppressed and how they were to be liberated, but votes, clearly, were a side issue. What really mattered to *The Freewoman* was how the so-called characteristics of women related to their oppression as a sex. Their maternal role, their domestic role; their sexual role, all their 'natural' roles were suspect and open to criticism. As stated by Caroline Boord:

Anyone who talks of Women's sphere is not truly 'Feminist' . . . the Free-woman wants no ready sphere . . . the Freewoman wants the whole round earth to choose from.
. . . it is a retrogressive idea to call any particular sphere or work 'Women's'. We do not know what women's work will be, we only know what it has been.
(*Freewoman* December 14, 1911:70)

The origins of women's oppression were murky and unclear and remained a 'moot point'. Dora Marsden was unsure whether it 'arose through the disabilities arising out of child bearing, or whether it arose through women giving up the game – i.e. bartering themselves for the protection of men' (*ibid*. November 23, 1911). What it resulted in was clear – the development of an unequal relationship between the sexes. 'For note, though some men might be servants, all women are servants, and all the masters are men. That is the difference and distinction. The servile condition is common to all women' (*ibid*.).

The original causes of women's oppression, according to Dora Marsden, were long gone, yet sex-bound roles continued. To her, and to many of her readers, these roles had to be abandoned if men and women were to be free. Whatever the origins of women's secondary position to men, Dora Marsden and others were convinced that it resulted in an oppressive sexual structure within contemporary society and an equally oppressive morality. Marriage, for example, was just another way of gaining protection from men and, in reality, was a form of prostitution – as Carpenter had argued (Carpenter 1896). In the first issue of *The Freewoman*, Edmund B. d'Auvergne had claimed that marriage had 'certain commercial advantages. By it the man secures the exclusive right to the woman's body and by it the woman binds the man to support her during the rest of her life . . . a more disgraceful bargain was never struck' (*Freewoman* November 23, 1911:5). If women were to be free, this, too, had to change.

Obviously, arguments such as these had radical implications for the issues of sexuality and reproduction. No contributor to *The Freewoman* advocated unlicensed promiscuity, but many did criticise the moral values that suffragists were so keen to uphold. Dora Marsden argued, in a series called 'The New Morality', that monogamous morality was

based on the intellectual apathy and insensitiveness of married women, who fulfilled their own moral ideal at the expense of the Spinster and Prostitute . . . indissoluble monogamy is an unjustifiable tyranny . . . it is blunderingly stupid and reacts immorally, producing deceit, sensuality, vice, promiscuity, prostitution, spinsterdom and a grossly unfair monopoly.

(*ibid.* January 4, 1912:121)

Marriage was 'a deliberate abrogation of freedom' backed by a law which was concerned 'with the rights of maintenance on the one hand and rights concerning sexual intercourse on the other'. It limited sexual expression while 'debasing female human being to the level of common merchandise' (*ibid.* June 20, 1912:81). Suffragists who demanded a reform of the institution were condemned since 'a prostitute would not haggle about her wares. Why then should a wife (or a suffragist)?' (*ibid.* February 8, 1912:221).

Writers and contributors to the paper even suggested new forms of relationship between men and women. Some felt that an exclusive relationship without a contract need not be oppressive, others argued that brief sexual encounters were not necessarily reprehensible. For example, Isabel Leatham thought that 'the Freewoman will not enter upon the sex relationship for any such conscious purpose as that of reproduction, but rather . . . will find passionate love between Men and Women, even if that be transient, the only sanction for sex intimacy' (*ibid.* January 11, 1912:151).

Free love unions were frequently proposed. They were supported by, among others, Guy Aldred and Rose Witcop who were themselves in such a union (Aldred 1956:62). Aldred could not understand why suffragists called for equality while, at the same time, they were uncritical of marriage whereby a woman lost her 'identity in that of a man by taking his name'; and his hope was that women would change the concept of their sex 'as an instrument of men's lust and put an end to man's power to send innocent girls and women on the road to prostitution, by daring to form free love unions, and preserving their own names, without fear or shame' (*Freewoman* January 18, 1912:179). In reply to happily married critics who emphasised the values of marriage and domesticity, Rose Witcop argued that she wanted them to become disgusted with the barrack like existence you are leading today, to fill your mind with thoughts higher than sex . . . to feel and think and live as you breathe – individually. But if your soul never wanders beyond the kitchen and the plush suite of furniture, even these ideas of freedom and discontent will certainly not meet with your approval.

(*ibid.* February 22, 1912:273)

This discussion developed into an affirmation of the sexuality of women and of their equal right to enjoy sex without conception. For example, d'Auvergne argued that 'sexual intercourse is not to be regarded as the preliminary to the production of children' (*ibid.* December 14, 1911:71), while another writer added that 'all natural functions require exercise, even when not employed on purely utilitarian purposes' (*ibid.* February 1, 1912:213). One vicar's wife claimed that most women 'give themselves for love', although 'there are women who disassociate the spiritual from the bodily appetite, and satisfy the latter without the former, just as a man can. There are some in fact, to whom it is a necessity of health to do so' (*ibid.* March 21, 1912:353). And a Freewoman Discussion Circle, comprised of a group of readers, went further and decided that celibacy for women, married or not, was simply unhealthy (*ibid.* August 8, 1912:270). Perhaps Stella Browne, an active socialist feminist who later founded the Abortion Law Reform Association in 1936 (Rowbotham 1977b), summed up the feeling of the majority of contributors when she wrote that 'the sexual experience is the right of every human being not hopelessly afflicted in mind or body and should be entirely a matter of free choice and personal preference, untainted by bargain or compulsion' (*Freewoman* March 21, 1912:354). Stella Browne also defended 'auto eroticism' (*ibid.* February 22, 1912:270), while other contributors defended homosexuality. In the series 'Uranians', Harry J. Birnstingl, for example, welcomed lesbianism within the women's movement and criticised discrimination against homosexuals (*ibid.* January 7, 1912:127; January 25, 1912:189).

Clearly, attitudes to sexuality in *The Freewoman* stood in marked contrast to those expressed in suffragist literature. Rank and file suffragists may well have discussed these issues, but their leaders took meticulous care to avoid any charges of immorality for fear of damaging the campaign for votes. This explains, for example, Millicent Fawcett's reaction to the paper and her avoidance of sharing a platform with Edward Carpenter (Strachey 1931:232–6). Yet the attitude of the suffragist leaders probably reflected a commitment to prevailing concepts of sexual morality too. Of course there were potential dangers for women in the relaxation of the moral code, but at least *The Freewoman* was willing to assess openly the relationship between contemporary sexual morality and the oppression of women. Tactical and other considerations seemed to prevent any kind of public debate on this issue within the major suffrage organisations: one WSPU member complained that in her organisation 'the great living principle of the world – sex – is beneath discussion. Is this to be our attitude when the vote is won? Surely we do not propose merely to force on men the standard they have forced on us. To do so would be to proclaim ourselves not merely slaves, but willing slaves' (*Freewoman* December 7, 1911:51).

The discussion on sex ran parallel with that on the issue of reproduction. Contraception was regarded as vital to the emancipation of women in terms of both their sexuality and their control of reproduction. Until women controlled their own fertility, most contributors argued, they could never be free. Indeed the role of 'passive maternity' had been instrumental in their subjection. The article, 'The Freewoman and The Birth Rate' (probably by Dora Marsden) stated that: 'The role of passive maternity combined with the economic dependence of women, which is its correlate, instead of leading to the respect for women by men . . . has had exactly the reverse effect' (*ibid*. November 30, 1911:36). The decision to have children should ultimately lie with women and should only be taken in their and their children's interests. Thus, at a time of growing concern over the size and health of the population, it was hoped that

feminist leaders, instead of attempting to explain away or apologise for the declining birth rate, will openly confess and glory in it and show what a magnificent future lies before humanity when women demand their right as mothers of the race to regulate their families in accordance with the possibilities of giving their children the best physical, mental and moral inheritance and environments.

(*ibid.*)

However, the basis on which contributors demanded the greater use and accessibility of contraception differed. The most obvious difference was between the Malthusians, led by C.V. Drysdale, and the Marxists. Drysdale argued that birth control was necessary to check the ever-expanding population from exhausting the world's finite resources; whereas the Marxists, although for contraception, felt that the unequal distribution of wealth, and not overpopulation, was the key to poverty. Nonetheless both groups saw the feminist implications of birth control. Drysdale, for example, claimed that 'one of the definitive advantages of prevention rather than continence is that it enables women to take the matter into their own hands' (*Freewoman* December 21, 1911:89).

Yet Drysdale's arguments often had eugenic undertones. In the same article he supported birth control for working class women, so as 'to improve the quality of the race by the refusal to propogate hereditary unfitness' (*ibid.*). To other contributors this was a limited argument and missed the point. Women must be able to choose freely or reject maternity on their own terms. Stella Browne made this clear in 'A Few Straight Questions To The Eugenics Society':

... for us Freewomen the issue is clear. We must secure a decent chance in the material environment for every child born into the world. We must see to it that the Woman who is passionately and pre-eminently maternal shall not be condemned to childlessness through economic pressure and mediaeval conventions, yet our right to refuse maternity is also an invulnerable right. Our wills are ours, our persons are ours.

(*Freewoman* August 1, 1912:217)

A major part of the debate on sex and reproduction constituted a direct attack on contemporary moral values. Some argued that here, too, there was 'one law for the rich, one for the poor . . . Adultery, a vice for the poor, is a pastime for the rich' (*ibid.* May 9, 1912:485). But this attack led to a ban on the open sale of the paper by W. H. Smith, the distributors – a ban that worried its editor, Dora Marsden and led her to curb the articles on women and sex (*ibid.* September 5, 1912:311). The courageous *Freewoman* was ultimately insisting that contemporary morality was hypocritical and that its ideals were prejudicial to the liberation of women.

In particular, the prevailing moral code further confirmed women in their domestic and maternal roles. Dora Marsden argued that the maternal role was a major cause of women's oppression.

To the door of the 'legitimate mother' and to the 'protection' accorded to her by popular sentiment, is to be traced the responsibility for most of the social ills from which we suffer. To her exemption from responsibility to earn her own livelihood in solid cash . . . is to be traced her incapacity to do so . . . it is therefore responsible . . . for the inadequate training, inefficient work, and consequent bad pay of women workers.

(*ibid.* January 11, 1912:154)

No contributor condemned motherhood *per se* but, like Dora Marsden and Stella Browne, most demanded a free choice for women.

Dora in particular welcomed motherhood, for married and unmarried women, and felt that women did have a unique relationship with their children. But she would have agreed with Ada Nield Chew's belief that motherhood, as it stood then, prevented women from gaining economic independence. In 'The Economic Freedom of Women', Ada Nield Chew argued that 'the greatest obstacle to economic freedom is the deeply rooted notion, in the minds of many of themselves, and in the minds of almost all men, that they are merely playing at work for a time until they undertake the "duties of wife and mother" ' (*ibid.* July 11, 1912:149). She added, as someone with 'many years trade union work among women workers' that this also prevented their organisation (*ibid.*). In 'Mother Interest and Child Training', Chew continued on this theme and wrote that 'women cannot live individual lives and develop on individual lines' if they are forced to become mothers and be dependent either on the state or on men (*Freewoman* August 22, 1912:270). In a statement that reveals her socialist background, she concluded that women would have to organise outside the home if they were to be emancipated. Again, this was especially difficult given the contemporary notion that the 'duties of wife and mother last from the moment a girl baby is born until she dies 70 years later, a grandmother' (*ibid.* July 18, 1912:169).

Both Ada Nield Chew and Dora Marsden considered that maternity leave should be granted to women workers who became mothers, and others condemned the idea that childcare was the unique province of women. For example, Edith Browne stated that 'it is just as absurd to expect every mother should want to play nursemaid to her baby as it used to be to insist that every woman must only do work of a domestic nature; that being her natural forte' (*ibid.* August 29, 1912:157). Dora Marsden added a further startling proposal: state-run nurseries for children of age two weeks and above. She admitted that this seemed drastic, but considered it necessary, for 'if women's work has to assume the permanent character of that of men, it must be of a permanent nature' (*ibid.* February 8, 1912:222).

H. G. Wells advocated the State Endowment of Motherhood (*ibid.* March 21, 1912:341), but editorial policy opposed this on the grounds that it confirmed a major aspect of the accepted role of women: in 'Woman: Endowed or Free', Dora Marsden argued that it would encourage 'the captivity of woman' and if the state was to pay women to become mothers why not pay them for their sexual services too? (*ibid.* February 29, 1912:281). It was hardly a sophisticated discussion of endowment and Dora felt 'we can effect bolder things' (*ibid.* March 21, 1912:342).

The discussion on motherhood and childcare ran in conjunction with an analysis of the domestic role of women. The domestic sphere as a vocation for women was heavily condemned. For example, 'Himander' (!) in their 'Fetish of the Domestic Sweat Shop', advocated an end to women's subjection to 'the 3 F's – Food, Furniture and Floors' (*ibid.* June 6, 1912:46). And Marsden's views were explained in a long article – 'The Drudge' (*ibid.* February 8, 1912:221–3): she deprecated housework as having no economic value and believed that the whole domestic role was outdated, serving only to restrict opportunities for women; she felt that modern women's work in the home, unlike that of their counterparts in pre-industrial days, was unproductive, and 'the modern housewife is a drudge because she creates nothing . . . yet after a century and a half of industrialism women are still fondly imagining their highest destiny is in "The Home" ' (ibid.:221).

This tradition, like so many others, had to be broken. Thus when the idea of creating a degree course in 'housewifery' at London University was mooted, the paper, in 'Notes of the Week', was aghast. Such a course, it was argued, was akin to one in 'The Current Modes of Teaching Pet Dog Fido Tricks' (ibid.:223); and the view of 'Educationalist' was that

The aims of those who frame such a retrograde scheme are in radical opposition to those of the women who are desiring the freedom and the development of women. They aim at perpetuating women's inferiority by perfecting her in a role which puts the greatest difficulties in the way of her development.

(Freewoman November 23, 1911:17)

This was the major criticism also levelled at the demand for wages for housework. Dora Marsden argued that such wages would confirm the domestic role and keep women dependent on men. She condemned Mrs Pankhurst and Olive Schreiner who (Dora claimed) had demanded an equal share in the wages of their husbands for housewives who stayed at home: to the editor of The Freewoman, these proposals were 'a striking indication of how short a distance the Woman Movement has travelled . . . [they] condone and suggest the abandonment of women's independent field of labour upon marriage and previsage the compulsory payment of wives by husbands, who will fill the role of employee and employer respectively' (ibid. February 8, 1912:222). As Dora later argued in 'Woman: Endowed or Free?': 'is the position of paid domestic servant the ideal of women in the emancipation movement?' (ibid. February 29, 1912:282).

If the domestic and maternal roles of women were oppressive, what was going to replace them? The Freewoman it seems, wanted 'the whole round earth to choose from' (ibid. December 14, 1911:70) and no fixed set of alternatives emerged. Some contributors, such as Fanny Johnson, felt that men and women should equally share housework and childcare. 'Might not the advice to go home and mind the baby sometimes be applied to the fathers?' Johnson asked (ibid. December 7, 1911:45). Others, including the organiser of the North West London Brent Garden Village scheme, A. Herbage Edwards, proposed 'group houses' where individuals would share the housework or employ professional domestic workers (ibid. March 7, 1912:312). Kathryn Oliver, ex-Secretary of the Domestic Workers Union of Great Britain, also suggested co-operative housekeeping (ibid. June 20, 1912:98).

The more radical analyses of marriage and the call for free love unions also implied the necessity of changes in the family structure. Certainly Guy Aldred, in his lecture to the Freewoman Discussion

Circle, 'Sex Oppression and the Way Out', was critical of the family. The report of the meeting claimed that 'his main point [was] that the existing social system, whose centre is the family, must be overturned before man can be freed from sex oppression, which is mainly due to the family system and the economic system' (*Freewoman* July 11, 1912:153). 'Brittomart' was also critical of 'the patriarchal family . . . with its subordination of the wife and child to the father'. She condemned Ramsay McDonald's recent defence of the family, and argued, echoing Engel's analysis, that as 'inheritance and property established the family . . . how it is going to persist under socialism is somewhat of a mystery' (*ibid.* January 11, 1912:151). Unfortunately there is little further evidence of discussion on the family although Guy Aldred's lecture was so popular that two more meetings on the same topic had to be arranged (*ibid.* July 25, 1912:194; August 8, 1912:224).

The Freewoman's prescriptions are not always clear but they do reflect the papers historical and theoretical importance. First, despite all the pressures to conform to gender-bound roles and a rigid standard of moral behaviour, revolutionary perspectives on sexuality, reproduction and the domestic and maternal ideology emerged. How many more are still 'hidden from history'? And, secondly, the discussion within the journal provided an acute and contemporary criticism of the major feminist positions within mainstream suffragism. Many suffragist arguments, *Freewoman* contributors claimed, were based on stereotyped roles that bore a direct relationship to the oppression of women, but the assumption within *The Freewoman* was that the liberation of women could only be achieved by the rejection of these roles.

Although the major function of *The Freewoman* was as a forum for debate, it did, in addition, organise one particular innovatory activity – The Freewoman Discussion Circles. These were designed to create further debate on the major issues raised in the paper. The idea was first suggested in February 1912 and the Bristol Fabian Women's Group proposed a network of local groups (*Freewoman* March 7, 1912:315). The first meeting was held at the International Women's Suffrage Shop in April but was so popular that the Circles had to move to larger premises. They were structured to allow discussion among the audience, and this was later facilitated by dividing into smaller groups (*ibid.* July 25, 1912:194). Topics discussed included celibacy, divorce, eugenics, prostitution, housework and Malthusianism. Detailed minutes of the meetings do not survive but the Circles' secretary, Barbara Low regularly reported their success in *The Freewoman*. Although they ceased with the collapse of the paper, the existence of the Circles is a further indication that contemporary feminism was by no means limited to the struggle for the vote.

But what of *The Freewoman*'s wider political analysis? How did the various contributors to the paper claim their goals were to be achieved? No one position was adopted, *The Freewoman* acting as a forum for revolutionary political currents, with socialism, Marxism, syndicalism and anarchism all represented within its pages. Dora Marsden once described herself as a 'philosophical anarchist' (*ibid.* August 19, 1912:295) and claimed that her political position was fluid as society itself was continually changing. The result was a vague editorial position which finally led H. G. Wells to complain to her that he did 'not believe you have any constructive ideas at all in your head, and that you do not know what you want in economic and social organisation, that the wild cry for freedom which makes me so sympathetic with your paper . . . is unsupported by the ghost of a shadow of an idea how to secure freedom' (*ibid.* September 5, 1912:312).

Nonetheless, both Marsden and her paper can be seen in the context of the contemporary revolutionary movement, partly as a result of their growing criticisms of parliamentary democracy and capitalism. Indeed, she argued that this revolutionary position was another reason for W. H. Smith's prohibition of the open sale of the paper (*ibid.* September 5, 1912:311). What was particularly striking about *The Freewoman* approach was its attempt, not always successful, to link the economic inequalities resulting from capitalism to the oppression of women. Allied to a growing sympathy with syndicalism, the debate within *The Freewoman* again contrasted sharply with the attitudes of suffragists who, after all, wanted to enter the political structure, not change it.

Broadly, *The Freewoman* condemned the inequalities of contemporary capitalism whereby, at its most basic level, 'in order that Many may have more, the Few will have to be content with less' (*ibid.* January 4, 1912:123). Arguing that labour alone created wealth, the discussion went on to examine the unequal distribution of the latter and the expropriation of surplus value, claiming that, at one factory, 'it is believed that every man and woman in the place have earned their wages by 11 o'clock' (*ibid.* January 11, 1912:144). In 'The Servile State', written during the turbulent summer of 1912, it was further argued that 'the sale of labour is the basis of immorality; it is the contradiction of freedom and it is the basis of capitalism', and the 'universal slavery of wage earners to capitalists' was condemned (*ibid.* June 6, 1912:41). 'The tendrils of cosmopolitan capitalism spread out North, South, East and West', and the paper called for 'the utter shattering and dissipating of the power of capital' (*ibid.* June 20, 1912:83).

Many writers argued that a parliamentary strategy was inadequate, especially in the struggle against capitalism, as Parliament itself was merely part of a superstructure that served the interests of capital.

In any community the politics of that community are a mere superstructure built upon the economic base . . . and even though Mr George Lansbury were Prime Minister and every seat in the House was occupied by Socialist deputies the capitalist system being what it is, they would be powerless to effect anything more than the slow paced reform of which the slow aim is to make 'men and masters' settle down in an uncomfortable and unholy alliance . . . The capitalists own the states. A handful of private capitalists could make England or any other country bankrupt within a week.

(*ibid.* August 8, 1912:222)

Certainly, many militants of the WSPU would have been shocked by the insistence that the 'kingdom of heaven has to be seized by force. A cross on a ballot paper will not do the deed' (*ibid.* August 8, 1912:222). They would have been appalled, too, at *The Freewoman*'s call for civil war, in December 1911, should Asquith not keep his promise and allow a women's suffrage amendment to the forthcoming Reform Bill. This was not to be

a thing of bags attached to strings containing stones, artfully directed against dead matter . . . but Civil War in the sense that it has made itself known to English History when men have risen to assert their rights of self government . . . and were prepared to drench their country in blood and behead a King!

(*ibid.* December 7, 1911:44)

The role of working class women in achieving 'the kingdom of heaven' was repeatedly emphasised. They were in fact urged to join a trade union rather than a suffrage society since, it was argued, the Labour movement more directly served their interests. Nonetheless, there was much criticism of the Labour Party and of the growing relationship of the Party with the NUWSS and WFL. In the context of calls to suffragists to ally themselves closely with the Labour Party, it was asked:

Could anyone ask a young movement to ally itself with so hopeless and hapless a baby as the Labour Parliamentarians? We think not. The Women's ranks have shown themselves far too liable to the same kind of disease as the Parliamentary Labour Party; the childish belief in Parliamentary action; the vain imagining that the masses do not count; that they are to be led up the Parliamentary stairs in fact.

(*ibid.* May 11, 1912:404)

The general consensus appears to have been that a women's movement should be built around working class women rather than around a particular political reform. In any case the suffragist demand for the vote on the same terms as men, was limited, for, as *The Freewoman* explained, 'Adult Suffrage [was] the only form of Women's Suffrage in which women workers would get any look in at all' (*ibid.* February 15, 1912:243). Women had 'lessons to learn; one – that the Parliamentary vote has not a tithe the power of concerted industrial action; two – that the organisation of women workers is a matter which should have proceeded pari passu with the demand for the vote' (*ibid.* May 11, 1912:404). Ada Nield Chew agreed that the suffrage societies over-emphasised the value of the vote: 'But after all, what can one expect to hope for? Each and all are governed and paid for by women who belong to a small and privileged class and she who pays the piper must surely call the tune?' (*ibid.* May 18, 1912:435).

Ada Nield Chew, with her many years of experience of trade union activity, was, however, very aware of the problems of organising working class women. She reminded other readers of the difficulties in doing this, although 'one of the best means . . . is to rouse a sense of resentment against obvious inequality, as in the voteless condition of women compared to men'. She knew the realities and the obstacles in the struggle for liberation and, as she put it, 'It will be a long business . . . 'Tis a long row to hoe' (*ibid.* April 18, 1912:435).

The importance of class was reinforced by Marxist contributors to the paper, the most prominent being Arthur D. Lewis. In a leading article, 'The Unimportance of the Woman's Movement', Lewis stressed the political limitations of suffragism and argued that

The Woman Movement is unimportant because it runs counter to well grounded reasoning. It talks about votes not property . . . It is useless for advocates of votes for Women to talk about low wages, prostitution, marriage and divorce. Women ought to have the vote as a matter of justice but the vote is of little use in remedying the evils usually referred to in speeches in favour of women's enfranchisement.

(*ibid.* January 11, 1912:147)

But Lewis's own brand of orthodox Marxism, with its emphasis on economic relations, had its drawbacks, too. Would economic equality alone bring the liberation of women? Isabel Leatham, for one, saw the importance of economic equality but warned that changes in the relationship between the sexes were also needed – without such changes 'it would be possible to have socialism with only a shadow of freedom for Women' (*ibid.* March 21, 1912:354).

Guy Aldred was well aware of Leatham's point. As a prominent figure in British anarchism, he was the leading exponent of syndicalism within *The Freewoman* forum, but also argued that liberation needed change in the relationship between men and women. Although stating 'our views are different . . . we are not communists; we are individualists' (*ibid.* August 8, 1912:253), Dora Marsden and one of her later co-editors, Grace Jardine warmly received Aldred's calls for a general strike and an industrial parliament. They described themselves as 'the most ardent supporters of the syndicalists in England' (*ibid.*), and also welcomed 'The Miners Next Step', a famous revolutionary document from South Wales miners (*ibid*. April 25, 1912:444). Indeed, they even argued that 'Socialism is an impossible form of society save with a servile people . . . men and women must have property. The individual must have property because, without it, he is not a complete human being' (*ibid*. August 29, 1912:281).

Marsden and Jardine were indeed individualists tinged, in Marsden's case especially, with religious and spiritual overtones. Just as Christabel Pankhurst became engrossed in religion, so did Dora Marsden who later wrote three incomprehensible books, *The Definition of the Godhead* (1928), *Mysteries of Christianity* (1930) and *The Philosophy of Time* (1955). This obsession was clearly evident in the early issues of *The Freewoman*, where she claimed that her task was to reveal the spiritual forces behind feminism (*Freewoman* November 30, 1911): the 'spiritual consciousness' would eventually 'constitute a higher development in the evolution of the human race and of human achievement'. However, it should be noted that religious and spiritual terms were common in the socialist and Labour movements of the time.

Simultaneously, an interest in humanism developed: by May 23, 1912, the paper had become *The Free Woman – A Humanist Weekly* whose aim was to resolve the struggle between 'feminism' and 'masculinism'. Humanism was hardly a theory that could include a class analysis and the editor's view of a forthcoming Golden Age, complete with a rustic return to the land must have disturbed many of the paper's radical supporters. The collapse and subsequent re-emergence of the paper as *The New Freewoman: An Individualist Review* in June 1913 emphasised its growing isolation and confusion. 'Women's Movement forsooth,' the new paper declared, 'Why does not someone start a straight nose movement . . . or any other movement based upon some accidental physical contournation?' (*New Freewoman* July 1, 1913:24).

It would be a mistake to exaggerate the size of *The Freewoman* distribution or its influence – Sharon Payne-Townshend, a Fabian married to George Bernard Shaw remarked that the paper was only 'a medium of self expression for a clever set of young men and women' (*New Freewoman* August 15, 1913:100). Nonetheless, the paper is crucial to an understanding of the early twentieth-century women's movement, if only by showing that the movement was not solely concerned with the vote. It presented a remarkable and contemporary criticism of the political and feminist limitations of suffragism – to most of its contributiors, the lack of the vote only reflected women's oppression, it did little to explain it. *The Freewoman* considered that the struggle for a single reform – the vote – diverted women's energies from wider feminist analyses. Thus, the debate in *The Freewoman* indicated the necessity for examining the sexual, as well as the political, status quo. Implicit in the discussion of women's roles as mothers, housewives and childcarers, and in the demand for a freer sexuality and control of reproduction, was the notion that liberation was not to be through parliamentary politics alone but through what amounted to an economic, social and sexual revolution.

Yet one problem remained unsolved. How could the revolutionary perspectives of the debate within *The Freewoman* be put into practice? How could they be transformed into a broadly based social and political movement? As Mary Gawthorpe wrote to Dora Marsden, 'a critical controversial paper . . . will always be in order and would ultimately be a blessing all round; but a critical movement postulates a pretty problem . . . Work it out sweetheart and let me know' (Mary Gawthorpe to Dora Marsden June 1, 1911).

6 From the Vote to Revolution: the East London Federation of Suffragettes to the Workers' Socialist Federation

Votes are, of course, just as important to working women as they are to working men, and the power of the vote is only limited by the power of the voters to use it well . . . Women who stay at home need the vote as much as the wage earners do, in order that they may see that good laws are passed for their homes and children.

(S. Pankhurst, *To Every Woman*, ELFWSPU 1913)

The Committee of the Workers' Socialist Federation places on record its belief that Parliament is an out of date reactionary body which should be abolished as soon as possible . . . The Socialist Revolution has spread from Russia to Germany, Austria and Bulgaria. The WSF wants that Revolution here; therefore it is promoting no Parliamentary candidates.

(Workers' Socialist Federation Executive Committee Report December 1918)

With their bourgeois trick of blaming everything on individuals or groups they are prone to lay the inequalities under which women have laboured through the centuries to the mere personal arbitrariness of men. 'Woman has been enslaved' say they 'by tyrant man'. This line of argument fosters sex antagonism; and sex antagonism hinders working class solidarity . . . The place of the working woman is with the vanguard of the proletariat marching in step with her working class brother.

(F. Conner, 'Working Women and the Class Struggle', *Workers' Dreadnought* August 13, 1921:6)

The East London Federation of Suffragettes had originally arisen out of the brief WSPU working class women campaign of 1912, when Flora Drummond and Sylvia Pankhurst agreed to rouse the women of the East End of London. The work was mainly left to Sylvia who began the campaign with the help and financial backing of the affluent Kensington, Chelsea and Paddington branches of the WSPU. She opened a headquarters at 321 Roman Road, Bow, and by May 1913 the East London Federation of the Women's Social and Political Union (ELFWSPU) was formed. The Federation united the newly created branches at Bow, Bromley, Stepney and Hackney (followed later by the addition of Canning Town), and was governed by a federation council which was composed of elected delegates from each branch and four honorary secretaries, including Sylvia and the treasurer, Norah Smyth (*Women's Dreadnought* March 8, 1914; January 2, 1915).

The uniquely democratic organisation of the Federation and its growing relationship with working class women led, as has been described, to the split away from the autocratic WSPU and, 'at the request of others' (*ibid.*), to the formation of an independent organisation, the East London Federation of Suffragettes (ELFS), in January 1914 (ELFWSPU Executive Minutes January 27, 1914). Growing co-operation with the Labour movement and the demand for adult suffrage alongside national aspirations led to the change in name – to the Workers' Suffrage Federation (WSF) – in February 1916. In turn, the Federation's involvement with the development of revolutionary socialism inspired the further change to the Workers' Socialist Federation (also referred to in the literature as WSF) in June 1918 (*Workers' Dreadnought* June 1, 1918:1014), and *The Women's Dreadnought*, the weekly paper of the ELFS and WSF became *The Workers' Dreadnought* in July 1917.

The WSF, as an integral part of the wartime revolutionary left, was involved in the negotiations that led to the birth of the British Communist Party. However, due to its opposition to Parliament – which was paradoxical given its suffragist background – and to affiliation with the Labour Party, its relationship with the Communist Party was stormy. The WSF itself, although declining in numbers, remained on the left of the Communist Party until the Federation's demise in 1924.

Sylvia Pankhurst's various organisations were small and their actual political influence should not be over-rated. In 1917, for example, Mrs Boyce, a provincial organiser, argued that the Federation could be seen merely as 'a charity society with suffrage tacked on' (General Meeting WSF January 15, 1917). *The Women's Dreadnought* was intended to have a weekly sale of 20,000, but surviving evidence indicates otherwise, even though Sylvia claimed that its circulation trebled during the War (General Meeting WSF September 18, 1916). Financially, Sylvia's organisations were continually in a precarious state, partly, of course, because a great many of their members were so poor themselves. Expenditure constantly outstripped revenue, and it appears that the Federations existed largely with the help of loans (see, for example, Finance Committee Minutes WSF 1917; 1918).

However, the WSF did have some national aspirations and by 1917, besides East London, there were 24 provincial branches in places as far apart as Portsmouth and Doncaster, Newcastle and Glasgow, and in London the Federation was further represented in Willesden, St Pancras, Kensal Rise, Golders Green and Islington (WSF Reports 1916–1917). Although born out of the women's suffrage movement, in no more than five years, Sylvia Pankhurst's organisations had developed a revolutionary socialism that was fundamentally opposed to the political assumptions of suffragism. What follows is an attempt to explain this process and its feminist implications.

Sylvia Pankhurst, like all the Pankhurst children, had been a suffragist all her thinking life (S. Pankhurst 1931), but one crucial difference between Sylvia and her mother and Christabel emerged during the suffrage campaign – her belief that votes would only come through mobilising the support of working class women. Sylvia's first major clash with the WSPU leaders over this issue arose out of their decision to end the brief working class women campaign of 1912. Sylvia wrote that she was 'determined that the East End work must go on' (*Women's Dreadnought* March 8, 1914:1), and in a guarded attack on Christabel,

> Some people tell us that it is neither especially important that working women should agitate for the Vote, nor especially that they should have it. They forget that, comparatively, the leisured comfortably situated women are but a little group, and the working women a multitude. Some people say that the lives of working women are too hard and their education too small for them to become a powerful force in winning the Vote, many though they are. Such people have forgotten their history.

> (*ibid.* March 21, 1914:3)

This conflict reflected a basic political difference between the autocratic attitude of both Christabel and Emmeline Pankhurst, and the democratic and ultimately socialist ELFS. Sylvia herself wrote of the 'fissure' between the two organisations – 'my relatives were moving to the right and I and our Federation to the left' (Pankhurst Papers, Amsterdam). The split of 1913 was also due to the growing links of the ELFS with the Labour and socialist movements. Christabel clearly wanted to disassociate the WSPU from working class organisations and would not tolerate the democratic structure of her sister's organisation. In an undated manuscript, 'The Women's Movement of Today and Tomorrow', Sylvia wrote that 'the ELF [was] expelled from the WSPU. I was sent to Paris where my sister was in hiding and told to inform our members that, owing to our democratic constitution, and because of our parent character, we must be put outside the proletarian body' (Pankhurst Papers, Amsterdam). Clearly, the WSPU leaders objected to 'mixing socialism with votes for women' ('The Inheritance', Pankhurst Papers, Amsterdam). They objected, too, to Sylvia's criticism of individualistic militancy, outlined in a circular to WSPU members in November 1913 (S. Pankhurst 1913). 'We will never win,' she wrote in her unpublished play 'Liberty or Death or A Popular Uprising For The Vote', 'until we have an army of men and women, marching with sticks and stones from the East End of London and other parts to make themselves terrible to this government' (Pankhurst Papers, Amsterdam).

Perhaps it was this threat, allied to a fear of losing votes to the Labour Party in the General Election scheduled for 1915, that lay behind Asquith's favourable reply to the ELFS deputation in June 1914. Although he never lost his own personal antipathy to votes for women, in this reply Asquith conceded: 'If the change has to come, we must face it boldly, and make it thorough going and democratic in its basis' (*Women's Dreadnought* June 27, 1914:57; Morgan 1975:131–2). It seemed to mark a significant change in Asquith's position; most suffragists, excluding the WSPU, and most of the Press saw it in this light (*Women's Dreadnought* July 4, 1914). But perhaps Asquith's emphasis on democracy rather than on women's rights was partly caused by a desire to appear unyielding to the Pankhursts' campaign.

In spite of its growing links with Labour and socialist circles the ELFS remained firmly committed to the vote; it was still essentially a suffragist organisation. Even though she had split from the WSPU, Sylvia denied that she was losing faith in votes for women; an article written in 1913 for *The Daily Herald*, 'A Storm In A Tea Cup and The Urgency Of The Vote' (Pankhurst Papers, Amsterdam), argued that women had an equal right to 'decide how the government shall be composed'. She even criticised 'men in the Herald movement who tell women that votes are out of date and useless [for] they themselves actually rely . . . on the power of the vote' (*ibid.*). The plight of many enfranchised men did not reflect the limitations of the vote, only their inability to use it wisely (*Women's Dreadnought* April 4, 1914). Indeed, 'the essential principle of the vote is that each one of us shall have a share of power' (*ibid.* March 21, 1914:3), while votes would increase the wages of women workers (*ibid.* April 4, 1914).

Although orthodox suffragist arguments were still evident in 1914, several distinguishing features of the ELFS were emerging. First, the Federation emphasised that the goals of working class women could only be won through their own activity – as Sylvia said at the launch of the Federation, 'we must get members to work for themselves and let them feel they are working for their own emancipation' (ELFS Executive Minutes February 25, 1914). Consequently, the campaign for votes had to be based on the realities of working class life in the East End:

our cue was to fan the flame of popular enthusiasm and to broaden our movement to take in even greater numbers and new sections . . . It was necessary, above all, to arouse the poor women of London, the downtrodden mothers whose lot is one dull grind of hardship in order that they may go in their thousands to demonstrate before the seats of the almighty.
(S. Pankhurst, *The Woman Movement of Today and Tomorrow*. Pankhurst Papers, Amsterdam)

Thus, instead of individualistic arson attempts on empty buildings, the Federation formed a 'People's Army' and suggested a 'No Vote, No Rent' strike. The army was originally intended to defend suffragette 'mice' against the 'Cat and Mouse Act' but it developed wider aims. The army, 'an organisation that men and women may join to fight for freedom and in order that they may learn to cope with the repressive methods of the Government's servants' (*Women's Dreadnought* March 8, 1914:2), was used in the 'free speech battles of 1914' (the ELFS had been banned from Public Halls in Bow, Bromley and Poplar), and Sylvia suggested that it could be used for 'trade disputes as well' (Sylvia Pankhurst to Captain White c. 1914).

In a leaflet encouraging East Enders to join the army, the militancy of the Federation compared with that of the WSPU became crystal clear. 'The only way to win votes for women is by fighting for it . . . the only way to meet the brutality of the Government is by armed resistance' (S. Pankhurst c. 1914a). The proposal of a rent strike, although not as dramatic as the WSPU's firing of Lloyd George's unfinished house in 1913, posed a far greater potential threat: the ELFS argued that it was 'the working woman's most powerful weapon', and the 'People's Army was to defend those that used it' (*Women's Dreadnought* March 21, 1914:8). Inevitably these tactics furthered links with Labour and socialist organisations particularly the Herald League, the ILP and the Marxist British Socialist Party (BSP) (*ibid.* March 21; March 28; May 6, 1914) – and the ELFS added red to the traditional green, purple and white of the WSPU (*ibid.* May 2, 1914:2).

Such developments positively identified the Federation as a class organisation. It still demanded the vote but, in contrast to the major suffrage societies, called for adult suffrage as 'the only possible demand of a working class movement' (ELFS Executive Minutes November 30, 1914). In 1914, Sylvia Pankhurst, on a hunger and thirst strike, still felt the vote was worth risking her life for, yet she had already privately admitted in late 1913: 'I am a Socialist and want to see the conditions under which our people live entirely revolutionised' (Sylvia Pankhurst to Captain White c. 1913). During the following years the ELFS was to question seriously whether or not the vote alone could achieve this.

The War was a crucial factor in the revolutionising of the ELFS. It sharpened economic and social differences within Britain and, by highlighting the inequality of sacrifice, pushed the Federation further beyond the political limits of suffragism. The Federation's growing opposition to the War also increased its contact with pacifist and revolutionary groups. Yet on the outbreak of the War the Executive Committee of the ELFS argued that it had three choices: '1. To carry on as if nothing had happened. 2. To try to make things better for those suffering from the War. 3. To make capital out of the situation' (ELFS Executive Minutes August 6, 1914). It opted for the second, although the third quickly followed.

Initially then, the ELFS concentrated on defending the interests of women in the East End. For example, it joined local committees for the relief of distress and demanded cheap food and free milk for mothers. It argued too that the food supply should be nationally controlled and at prices 'fixed by working women' (*Women's Dreadnought* August 15, 1914:85). The Federation further urged the Government to provide work 'for men and women at Trade Union rates; women to be paid equal rates', to enforce a moratorium on debts and rents and to put 'working women . . . on all committees for fixing food prices and for providing employment and relief' (*ibid.*). The Federation also campaigned for regular and adequate separation allowances for soldiers' and sailors' wives (S. Pankhurst 1932).

What these demands, made in August 1914, amounted to was a fierce determination not to aid the war effort but to protect the working class community in the East End. They stressed class interest even during the worst excesses of national and patriotic fervour. At the same time, however, they had clear (and practical) feminist implications. Two particular projects, the Toy Factory and 'The Mothers' Arms', illustrate this well. The Toy Factory was established to give employment to working class mothers. They were paid the minimum male rate of a pound a week in contrast to the ten shillings at the Queen Mary Workshops (Toy Factory file, Amsterdam). A creche was provided which proved so popular that an old pub was set up as a working nursery – 'The Mothers' Arms' – with the old bar room converted into the 'Mothers' Reception Room'. Children aged from one month to five years were taken, the fees were low and a doctor attended regularly. There was even a nursery school, using the advanced Montessori method (*The Mothers' Arms*, WSF 1915).

These projects, along with the Federation's cheap cafe and milk centres (*Women's Dreadnought* August 29, 1914:94; September 5, 1914:97) can be seen to reflect Sylvia's feminism which was firmly rooted in working class concerns. In 1915 she argued for 'Free Public Nurseries . . . to accommodate all the children whose mothers are obliged to leave them there, either regularly, because their mothers are wage earners, or occasionally because the mother is ill, or for some other cause' (*ibid.* November 6, 1915:356); and she also argued for 'communal restaurants, supplying first rate food at cost price [to] emancipate the mother from the too multifarious and often hugely conflicting labours of the home' (S. Pankhurst 1932:43). These demands may well have been based on an apparent acceptance of the sexual division of labour, but nonetheless they were directly related to the reality of women's lives in the East End of London.

The Federation's practical response to the War furthered its class orientation. Acting in contrast to the jingoism of, for example, the WSPU, the ELFS called on landlords to show their patriotism by lowering rents (*Women's Dreadnought* August 22, 1914:90). It also demanded fair wages for women war workers, stating that 'there is nothing patriotic in working at sweated rates to pile up profits for Government contractors' (*ibid*. October 10, 1914:119). In particular, the Federation was quick to denounce upper class jingoists such as Lady Frances Balfour who dismissed those women who complained about rising prices 'as deserving of being treated as deserters as ever any soldier who runs from the rifle fire of the entrenched position he has to take' (*ibid*. August 29, 1914:95). Such sentiments could hardly have impressed East End women faced with rising prices and reduced incomes. One woman, with five children and another on the way, itemised her budget which was weekly in deficit: 'We are eating less, and have pawned away many things to make up the difference, but that can not go on' (S. Pankhurst 1932:128–9).

It was this reality that fostered class antagonism and the socialist perspectives of the ELFS. Orthodox suffragist political analysis and patriotism were linked in that they both denied class conflict – the latter by stressing the 'national interest' – but the ELFS, based in an impoverished working class community, had already begun to question this – and the War speeded up the process. As early as August 1914, Sylvia had warned of the dangers of jingoism, adding that 'it is practically certain that every war of modern times has been fought with the purely materialistic object of forwarding the schemes and protecting the interests of the powerful and wealthy financiers' (*Women's Dreadnought* August 1, 1914:78). She was to add that they were fought 'as a rule, for commercial objects, for the acquisition of valuable markets and territory' (*ibid*. October 3, 1914:114).

These arguments developed into a socialist analysis of the War and in December 1914, *The Women's Dreadnought* published the German Marxist Liebnicht's view that it was 'an imperialist war, a war for the rule of the world market' (*ibid*. December 26, 1914:164). Melvina Walker had stressed that the 'working class do not want war', and Sylvia had intended to organise opposition from the beginning (*ibid*. August 15, 1914). But Sylvia realised that she 'could not say much against the war at present as so many people have relations in it, that they will not listen yet' (ELFS Executive Minutes August 6, 1914).

Increasing numbers did begin to listen as the War dragged on, poverty and hardship increased and civil liberties declined. And many of the issues that arose out of the War strengthened links with socialist and pacifist organisations. One such issue was the Government's attempt to aid 'National Service' by creating a national register of adults. As far as Sylvia was concerned, this was only geared towards helping those 'powerful and wealthy private individuals who are piling up enormous war profits' (*ibid.* June 12, 1915:262) and was the forerunner to the enforced conscription of labour (*ibid.* August 14, 1915:299). A joint demonstration, with various unions, the Herald League, some ILP branches and the Marxist BSP, was made against the proposed register. Campaigns over free speech, the food supply and sweated industries brought further contact with such groups, and by 1915 the Federation claimed that its speakers had 'addressed a large number of Suffrage, Socialist, Trade Union and Labour organisations throughout the country' (ELFS Annual Report 1915).

The ELFS was thus becoming not only more revolutionary, but less parochial too. This was reflected in the change of name to the Workers' Suffrage Federation in 1916, and in the increasing national coverage within *The Women's Dreadnought*. Thus, although still demanding votes and still active in the East End, the Federation reported on, and supported, the militant class struggles of miners in South Wales (*Women's Dreadnought* September 4, 1915:310–12) and shipworkers on the Red Clyde (*ibid.* January 8; April 18, 1916). The growth of provincial branches (often set up with the help of local ILP and BSP contacts) in Birmingham, Durham and Leeds (ELFS Executive Minutes March 6; May 1; May 8, 1916) further reflected the national character of the new revolutionary organisation.

In fact, the Federation had become an integral part of the growing revolutionary opposition to the War. Besides organising lectures on pacifism, Marxism and international socialism (*Women's Dreadnought* October 14, 1916:570) it portrayed the War as something from which the working class stood to gain nothing. Conscription was regarded as a mere device to create cheap, obedient labour and cannon fodder (*ibid.* November 20, 1915:365). The War and conscription together were seen as having little to do with a fight for liberty, but as 'a means of making the few richer and the many poorer and a means also of forging chains by which those who work can be more firmly controlled by those who profit by their labour' (*ibid.* August 7, 1915:294).

Sylvia Pankhurst had openly declared her belief in collectivism as early as July 1915 – not the collectivism of the state in wartime but of socialism. 'I believe in collectivism' she wrote in an article criticising the Government's national register 'in the collective action of free people agreeing on equal terms to subordinate the separate individual wishes for the benefit of the whole . . . [in the proposal for the register] I see not the collective action of a free people for the common welfare, but the enslavement of the many for the profit of the few' (*ibid.* July 24, 1915:286). She added later in 1915 that 'the only bulwark against the exploitation of capitalists is the organised intelligent solidarity of the working class' (*ibid*. December 4, 1915:372). Sylvia had already begun to read Marx by this time for 'all those who attacked the ethics of present society at its base took on a deeper meaning' (S. Pankhurst 1932:69).

It seemed a long way from votes for women. But the ELFS and the Workers' Suffrage Federation remained committed to the vote, albeit the reason for that commitment differed from orthodox suffragism: the Federation's demand for votes for women, from 1914 to 1916, formed part of its demand for adult suffrage. The Federation emphasised this as a class issue and strenuously campaigned for support for adult suffrage among Labour and socialist circles. It convened a Joint Committee for Adult Suffrage and organised an Adult Suffrage Conference in Leicester at the end of 1916, with representatives from over 34 socialist and Labour organisations (*Women's Dreadnought* December 2, 1916:607), and continued to press for adult suffrage throughout most of 1917.

When allied to its criticism of the state and of the War, it became clear that the battle for the vote was only part of a much wider struggle. Old suffragist sentiments that the vote was needed to 'safeguard the interests of the Women, nay, the race' (*ibid*. December 19, 1914:164) became infrequent, and it was stressed, as Sylvia put it, that 'the battle for human suffrage is part of the great struggle for upward human evolution, in the course of which dominance and compulsion, exploitation and poverty will be abolished' (*ibid*. January 22, 1916:408). Although Sylvia stressed the importance of the vote to the Leicester Conference in 1916, perhaps her true feelings were expressed in a statement made two months earlier: 'We are tired of the Suffrage Movement, it must be settled once and for all in order that we may move on to things which will carry us further forward in the evolution of progress' (*ibid*. October 14, 1916:568).

Reactions to the international and national events of 1917 and 1918 finally ended the WSF's waning commitment to liberal democracy; the Russian Revolution spurred on revolutionary socialists throughout Europe; in Britain, class struggle, inspired both by the War and by the news from Petrograd and Moscow, reached new heights. In British industry, as dilution increased and wages declined, illegal strikes multiplied – in May 1917 alone, one and a half million working days were lost. In the Clyde, Yorkshire and in South Wales, industrial militancy reached new levels and, in June 1917, the famous Leeds Soviet Convention called for the inauguration of British Soviets, and of councils of workers' and soldiers' delegates. Mutinies in the army and navy increased, and the War Office began to doubt the loyalty of rank and file troops in the event of revolution (Kendall 1969).

It was in this context that the Federation's transformation from suffragism to revolutionary socialism was completed. Thus while still calling for adult suffrage, the Annual Conference of the WSF in May 1917 declared that 'the capitalist system of society is irreconcilable with the freedom and the just demands of the workers', and it urged the Federation 'to work for the abolition of that system and the establishment of a Socialist Commonwealth in which the means of production and distribution shall be employed in the interests of the people' (*Women's Dreadnought* June 2, 1917:766). Two months later, in Carmarthen, South Wales, Sylvia called for 'immediate peace on the basis of no annexations, no indemnities, Adult Suffrage, the abolition of the House of Lords and the substitution of an industrial Parliament' (*ibid.* July 14, 1917:802). This was hardly compatible with the orthodox suffragist acceptance of parliamentary democracy, and was perhaps a logical outcome of the Federation's emphasis on class and its attitude to a war which was 'being waged in the interests of the capitalists and is antagonistic to the Workers of the World' (*ibid.* June 2, 1917:766).

The Russian Revolution must be seen as crucial to the development of the Federation's revolutionary socialism. The WSF realised the importance of the March revolution and its support went beyond the general approval in the English Press of the fall of Tsarism: it criticised the pro-War policy of the new Provisional Government and argued that the real revolutionaries were in the Soviets (*ibid.* March 24, 1917). It sent best wishes 'to the Russian workers in the great fight which they have made and are making for freedom and democracy' and expressed the 'hope that an early election may result in the return of an overwhelming majority of class conscious representatives of the workers' (WSF General Members Meeting March 19, 1917). However, this lingering faith in parliamentary elections in effect clashed with other positions of the WSF platform, particularly its support of workers' and soldiers' councils (*Women's Dreadnought* June 9, 1917:773).

But what little commitment to parliamentary democracy remained was finally ended by the Bolshevik Revolution in November. The Bolsheviks had seized control from Kerensky's Provisional Government and had agreed to participate in the elections to a Constituent Assembly. But, despite their powerful position, they failed to achieve a majority and this exposed, to Sylvia, the weakness of electoral parliamentary strategies. In an article, 'What About Russia Now?', Sylvia argued that the result tended to support

the Syndicalists, Industrial Unionists or simply Marxian socialists . . . who believe that Parliaments, as we know them, are destined to pass away into the limbo of forgotten things, their places being taken up by organisations of the people built up on an occupational basis. The failure of the elections to the Constituent Assembly, even though they were decided by adult suffrage ballot, to return members to support the policy of the Soviets is strong evidence that the industrialists have found the true path.

(ibid. January 26, 1918)

Not surprisingly, the limited measure of votes for women in early 1918 was met with indifference, if not hostility, by the WSF and the Federation held aloof from rejoicing at this 'victory'. 'Saddened and oppressed', wrote Sylvia, 'by the great world tragedy, by the multiplying graves of men, the broken hearts of women, we hold aloof from such rejoicings; they strike us with a hollow and unreal sound upon our consciousness' *(ibid.* February 16, 1918:948). The crucial question was no longer votes, nor even adult suffrage, but it was socialism and how to achieve a socialist society. Clearly, Parliament had little to do with this.

Very robust must be our faith in the possibility of re-creating the dry, crumbling bones of Parliament, and of filling its benches with vigorous uncompromising Socialists, determined to take immediate action to sweep away . . . Capitalism, and to establish Socialism in our time. Is it possible to establish Socialism with the Parliament at Westminster as its foundation?

(ibid.)

Obviously, the WSF's answer was 'no': in Parliament's place should be 'a local, national and international system, built up on an occupational basis, of which the members shall be but the delegates of those who are carrying on the world's work . . . drawn from the bench, the desk, the kitchen and the nursery' *(ibid.).*

The Federation became the Workers' Socialist Federation in June 1918. Significantly, both the reference to women and to suffrage had been dropped. The new WSF, born out of the suffrage movement but now far removed from it, was dedicated to the overthrow both of the parliamentary system and of the economic structure the Federation felt it served. The inaugural Conferences of the Workers' Socialist Federation agreed that

the Government and the State are institutions for the specific purpose of protecting private property and perpetuating wage slavery, [and the WSF] pledges itself to work for the abolition of the capitalist system as the paramount question of immediate importance. It considers that Parliament organised on a territorial basis and government from the top are suited only to the capitalist system.

(Workers' Dreadnought June 1, 1918:1014)

It urged the working class to 'organise on an industrial basis and to build up a National Assembly of Local Workers' Committees, directly representing the workers which shall render Parliament unnecessary by usurping its functions' *(ibid.).*

Although women had fought for the vote for years, the post-War

General Election only interested the WSF as a propaganda exercise. It argued that the election only 'interests us so far as it can be made a sounding board for the policy of replacing capitalism with socialism and Parliament by the Workers' Councils. We shall be at the elections but only to remind the workers that capitalism must go' (*Workers' Dreadnought* November 2, 1918:1106). The proposal to allow women MPs in the new Parliament was criticised as a gimmick, a cheap attempt to popularise a useless institution. The WSF expected little from women in the Commons since they considered that 'they will go and play the old Parliamentary game that achieves so little' (*ibid.*). On the occasion of the very first election in which women could vote, Sylvia Pankhurst, who had in 1914 risked her life for women's suffrage, summed up the Federation's position: 'we hope for nothing in this election, save that it might serve to spur the workers to abolish Parliament, the product and instrument of the capitalist system' (*Workers' Dreadnought* December 14, 1918:1152).

The WSF's virulent opposition to parliament and parliamentary activity (in fact, a kind of extreme but revolutionary anti-suffragism) continued until its demise in 1924 and became a major stumbling block in the negotiations that led to the formation of the Communist Party of Great Britain in August 1920. In fact the WSF adopted the title 'Communist Party' in June 1919 with a programme against parliamentarianism and against affiliation with the Labour Party, although it postponed using the name pending further negotiations with other left-wing groups (*ibid.* June 14; June 21, 1919). Sylvia withdrew from the negotiations over these issues (and over her editorial control of *The Workers' Dreadnought*), and formed her own Communist Party (British Section of the Third International) in June 1920 (*Workers' Dreadnought* – 'Organ of the Communist Party' – July 3, 1920:1).

Under pressure from Lenin, whom she went to meet with Willie Gallacher, in 1920, Sylvia agreed to merge with the Communist Party of Great Britain and the two joined in January 1921. However, refusing to relinquish control of *The Workers' Dreadnought*, wary of the new discipline within the party, and still critical of any parliamentary strategies, she was forced to leave the Party in September 1921 (*Workers' Dreadnought* January 15; September 17, 1921; Pelling 1958; Kendall 1969). 'By far the most accomplished and apocalyptic journalist and orator of the extreme left' was doomed to the political wilderness (D. Mitchell 1970:755).

The history of Sylvia Pankhurst's contribution to the revolutionary movement in Britain is yet unwritten and requires a separate study. Given her suffragist background, her unswerving criticism of any revolutionary strategy that involved Parliament was remarkable. And, in spite of pressure from Moscow and Lenin's specific criticisms of her 'intellectualist childishness' in his *Left Wing Communism: An Infantile Disorder* (1950 ed.:69), Sylvia stood her ground.

The arguments and activity of the new Workers' Socialist Federation in the years from 1918 to 1920 tended to submerge discussion of the oppression of women. The political analysis of the Federation during the War had appeared to imply that the oppression of women was a question of class rather than of sex. As 'Comrade George J. Cohen' had written in *The Women's Dreadnought*, 'is it a question of sex or class oppression? Remember we are not oppressed as men or women . . . or as black, white, or yellow people. We are oppressed internationally as a working class' (*Women's Dreadnought* January 13, 1917:649). This orthodox Marxism was increasingly common within the paper and was probably reflected in its change to *The Workers' Dreadnought* in July 1917. It was reflected, too, in the change, a few months earlier, to the Workers' Suffrage Federation and its opening of membership to men. The liberation of women no longer required a separate women's organisation and could (it also seemed) be achieved through revolutionary economic change alone. Yet neither Sylvia Pankhurst nor the WSF ignored the specific oppression of women and this remained clear throughout the War and the 1920s. But how successful were they in identifying or explaining the relationship between their feminism and their socialism?

Much of the Federation's feminism was directed towards meeting the practical needs of women in the wartime East End. The Toy Factory, 'The Mothers' Arms', the milk centres and the cheap cafe, all remained an important part of the Federation's work, accounting for a large part of its budget throughout the War (WSF Finance Committee Minutes 1917). Birth control was also on the agenda: Miss Bonwick, for example, gave talks on 'The Woman's Right to Know' as early as March 1914, followed by a lecture on the need for children's sex education (*Women's Dreadnought* March 8, 1914:3; July 18, 1914:71). It seems that these topics were discussed further by others until at least 1916, if not beyond that date (*ibid.* December 2, 1916:609). The Malthusian League's recent pamphlet *Family Limitation Doctrine* was also frequently advertised (*ibid.* December 30, 1916:638).

The Federation's attitude towards women and reproduction was practically oriented rather than daringly radical in the manner of *The Freewoman*. Perhaps its position was most clearly outlined in Sylvia Pankhurst's response to the Report of the Royal Commission on the Birth Rate of 1916 (quoted in *Women's Dreadnought* July 8, 1916:506). Brushing aside myths of motherhood ('at best each birth brings to the working class mother a heavy load of care and contriving'), Sylvia argued that the Report painted a 'gloomy picture' and showed 'the need of the mother for peace from the strain of pregnancy and child bearing' (*ibid.*). She was horrified by Dr Mary Sharlieb's allegation that 'in the working classes there are five abortions to every live birth', and gave a guarded welcome to Dr Drysdale's recommendation for a wider use of birth control. She was dubious, though, of the argument that working class life could be improved solely by contraception and control of the population, as Drysdale, Secretary of the Malthusian League, implied. To Sylvia Pankhurst the nub of the problem was 'the capitalist system, with its appalling extremes of poverty' (*ibid.*).

Here, then, was a practical response to the problem of reproduction, influenced by the reality of life in the East End. A more libertarian approach would have been difficult to pursue in the middle of 1916, even though Sylvia appeared to hold the view that sex itself was not purely for procreation. She argued, too, that the whole problem was complicated by 'the economic dependence of the mass of women', but added, typically, that 'to poor people [it] is infinitely more difficult than to the rich' (*ibid.*). So, although the special position of women was not ignored, the assumption was that it was ultimately a question of class and capitalism, not sex and men's power over women. The link between the two was not fully explored and the solution to women's oppression remained the socialist commonwealth.

Concern over particular aspects of women's oppression was reflected in the WSF's virulent criticism of DORA (*Workers' Dreadnought* April 6, 1918:980), as well as in Sylvia's views on women's work in the home, which she clarified during a tour of the South Wales coalfields in 1917. Clearly, 'mine owners enjoy affluence because of the miners' toil' but the miners themselves were 'dependent upon the women who cook their meals, wash their clothes and clean their homes. Not merely their comfort but their earning capacity is increased by the labour of these women' (*ibid.* October 13, 1917:864). While supporting the miners in their campaign for a shorter working week, Sylvia reminded them that 'the housewives' work is never done!' (*ibid.*). She recommended communal cafes, the sharing of housework and the creation of mothers' institutes. She envisaged better and cleaner homes which, if not provided by the current system, were 'another reason for working to secure Socialism' (*ibid.*).

Sylvia's criticism of the sexual division of labour was primarily economic – the toil of the miners' wives was essential to the profits of the mine owners. But she identified this without explaining men's power over women. In fact feminist arguments within the WSF were increasingly based on the notion that 'women's wrongs are men's wrongs. Capitalism is the common enemy of both sexes and can only be destroyed by both sexes in co-operative action' (*Workers' Dreadnought* September 22, 1917:857). Certainly by 1918 the WSF appeared 'to assume that feminism would simply become part of the revolutionary movement' (Rowbotham 1977a:160).

Nonetheless a discussion of how the revolution would particularly benefit women emerged in the 1920s (*Workers' Dreadnought* November 4, 1922, July 7, 1923). In particular, some of the old functions of the family would be removed or socially organised. Communal restaurants, laundries and clothes-mending shops would be augmented by professional houseworkers, while the needs of children would be met by the state. This would in turn alter sexual relationships for 'men and women may marry, simply because they love each other, without any regard whatsoever to the economic burdens or social conventions. These will have disappeared' (*ibid*. January 10, 1920). These views reflected opinions of the revolutionary Russian feminist, Alexandria Kollantai, whose *Communism and The Family* was published by the WSF in 1921. The discussion in *The Workers' Dreadnought* however, emphasised economic causes and solutions to women's oppression, and Kollantai's wider views on communism, sex and love were not discussed (Rowbotham 1974).

Towards the last years of the WSF in 1924, however, Sylvia Pankhurst did begin to ponder sex and morality. In 'Sex and Parentage', for example, she wondered whether the

sexual attraction of men and women will in the future tend to dwindle towards extinction, having been artificially inflated by the private property system and consequently the economic subjection of Women as the sex handicapped by maternity; or whether its extension beyond the mere purpose of reproduction is an essentially human characteristic which is destined to become strengthened and ennobled in the course of evolution and to be enhanced and enriched with the advent of the dawn of plenty.

(*Workers' Dreadnought* March 8, 1924:1–3)

She added 'the latter is our own view'. 'Conceptions of morality,' Sylvia continued, 'are changing quantities built up and modified in conformity with social conditions . . . when sex is freed from economic considerations . . . it will be found to live up to a good reputation at least as fully as it has often been thought to deserve a bad one' (*ibid*.). (Sylvia herself, although no sexual libertine, had a long-standing relationship with the Italian anarchist Silvio Corio, by whom, in 1927 and at the age of 45, she had a son, Richard Keir.)

This last article appeared four months before the paper folded and Sylvia's temporary retirement from politics. (Her political activity was to resume in the struggle against Italian fascism.) Serving teas to weekend visitors in her 'Red Cottage' near Epping Forest in 1924 seems to have been a curious finale to the career of Sylvia Pankhurst, suffragette and revolutionary.

Perhaps the most important aspect of the ELFS and the WSF was their exposure of the limitations of suffragism. Simply put, they argued that women, even voting women, could never be equal in an economic system that was based on inequality – inequality that was not difficult to demonstrate in the East End of London. The War made such inequality even greater although the break with suffragism can be seen, with hindsight, to have begun with the split with the WSPU leadership in 1913. The emphasis on the potential power of working class women obviously clashed with the strategy and analysis of Christabel and Emmeline Pankhurst and, together with the reactions to the War, was to lead to the platforms of 1917 and 1918.

However, in this process (and in spite of the relief work in the East End), the feminist theory of the WSF was often submerged in the development of a Marxist analysis of the exploitation of the worker under capitalism. Nor was the argument with other revolutionary groups in the years from 1918 to 1920 about the oppression of women, but rather about the role of Parliament, affiliation with the Labour Party and control of *The Workers' Dreadnought*. Although the WSF continued to make specific demands for women and Sylvia Pankhurst began, as has been described, to reconsider their sexual oppression, yet the power of men, as a sex, over women was not fully explained – it was considered that emancipation for both sexes would come through class struggle and the establishment of socialism. Such views clearly had important practical and theoretical ramifications. Sylvia herself did not seem to contemplate 'the possibility of feminism being overpowered and subsumed within a male dominated revolutionary movement' (Rowbotham 1977a:160) and seemed to think sexual equality would accompany the revolution by the working class as a whole. The WSF may well have indicated the inequalities of capitalism and of parliamentary democracy but it still left many dilemmas unresolved.

7 Suffragists, Militancy, War or a Substitute for Revolution? Why were women given the vote?

If the change has to come, we must face it boldly, and make it thorough going and democratic in its basis.
(Asquith to Sylvia Pankhurst's East End Deputation June 20, 1914; quoted in
Women's Dreadnought June 27, 1914:57)

[As the law] began to interfere in the home . . . and the health of the people and the education of their children . . . it was inconceivable that half the population, and especially that half of the population which was most concerned with the home . . . should have absolutely no voice at all in determining what was to be done.
(Lloyd George to suffragist deputation March 29, 1917; quoted in Harrison
1978:135)

I suggest that the vote is granted nowadays on no grant of fitness, but as a substitute for riot, revolution and rifle. We grant the suffrage in order that we may learn in an orderly and civilized manner what the people who are governed want.
(Earl Russell, House of Lords December 17, 1917; quoted in Harrison
1978:220)

The argument that women should not be excluded from voting in parliamentary elections was finally accepted in 1918. It had been a long struggle which went back as far as 1832 – and it was still not over. Fear of creating a majority of women voters had led to an age limit of 30 years, an obstacle not removed until 1928. Why did women have to wait for the vote until after the First World War? What contribution did each of the major suffrage organisations make towards the success of 1918? A brief consideration of these questions will contribute to an understanding of the campaign and further challenge some persistent misconceptions about suffragism as a whole.

There have been numerous explanations of why the vote was gained in 1918. Many emphasise the War and women's warwork (C. P. Hill 1977:234; Hussey 1971:239, 277); others the importance of changes – for example in the education and employment of women – that had taken place before the War began (Fulford 1957:298–9). Some have considered both factors; and most of them, of course, give varying degrees of credit to the suffragist campaign itself. But, by the overriding emphasis on the WSPU, the contribution of the suffragettes to the victory of 1918 has been over-rated. Indeed, such emphasis has left a legacy which implies that the suffrage movement was synonymous with the Pankhursts and that they alone were responsible for its success.

Moreover, by reducing the great mass campaign to a mere battle of wills between Asquith and the WSPU leaders, this view has also over-rated the importance of the replacement, in 1916, of Asquith by the pro-suffragist Lloyd George. Further, it has left an impression that the Coalition Government of 1917 and 1918 was influenced by the threat of renewed suffragette militancy. As has been described, what remained of the WSPU by that date was in no condition to resurrect the tactics of 1913 and 1914 even if it had wanted to: in fact, Christabel's main concern was pursuing the war effort and fighting the menace of socialism.

A major distortion in many accounts of the gaining of the vote is the weight given to the change in 'public opinion' caused by women's warwork. The very concept of 'public opinion' is nebulous and notoriously difficult to establish. It is also open to influence by powerful interests, in particular, the media. For example, *The Times* carried many glowing articles on women war workers – because Lloyd George asked Lord Northcliffe to help him overcome opposition to women's suffrage within the cabinet (Pugh 1978:146). Nonetheless, this does not mean women's work was not important in influencing opinion: it challenged some of the old myths, particularly with regard to female physical capabilities: women had, of course, always worked in hard and dangerous jobs but it was not until the war effort that their ability to do so was publicly recognised. The irony of the 1918 Act was that the 30-years age limit prevented many women workers, so highly praised for their contribution to the War, from getting the vote. Some had to wait until 1928.

However, the war was crucial to the suffragists' ultimate success but in a far more complex way than by merely changing some men's attitudes towards women. In particular, it removed many of the political obstacles to women's suffrage that had existed before 1914. Then, the suffrage campaign had floundered on party suspicions and relationships, on its interaction with other political issues as well as on the personal opposition of the Prime Minister. It had aroused hostility, too, among those opposed to any move towards universal suffrage (Close 1977), while a major concern of the political parties was that 'the balance' between them would be upset.

This was, in fact, a parliamentary euphemism – it meant that each party would only support a measure that would not endanger its prospects of electoral success. Thus, those Tories not opposed to women's suffrage would only support a limited measure; suffragist Liberals and Labour candidates, a wide one. Fear of the possible effect of electoral reform on party representation in Parliament was also behind the Irish Nationalists' opposition to votes for women: they were frightened that a change in the franchise would lead to a customary reorganisation of parliamentary seats and a possible reduction in the Irish presence at Westminster. Neither did the 'Nats' wish to upset Asquith's Government since they felt it offered the best chance of Home Rule – so, in crucial votes on women's suffrage, the Irish Nationalists abstained.

The House of Lords with its inbuilt Tory majority presented the greatest opposition to Liberal franchise reform. The Lords had been a thorn in the Liberals' side since the general Election of 1906. The Upper House had obstructed various Liberal proposals, including those on licensing, education and plural voting, before the famous crisis over the People's Budget of 1909. Clearly, the Peers' influence had to be curbed, and Asquith invited the Liberal Party in 1908 'to treat the veto of the House of Lords as the dominating issue in politics' (Koss 1976:106). Yet even after the General Elections of 1910 and the Parliament Act of 1911 (which did curtail the power of the House of Lords), the suffragist chances of success were still slim. The Liberals were wary of risking another election which traditionally followed franchise reform at a time when there was a whole series of complex and controversial bills, ranging from Home Rule to National Insurance, pending in an overcrowded parliamentary timetable. With a lack of consensus between (or even within) the parties, a divided cabinet, a hostile Prime Minister and Tory bitterness over the Parliament Act, a suffragist in 1911 'could almost be forgiven for being defeatist' (Morgan 1975:78).

The War radically altered this hopeless picture. It gave the appearance of consensus among the parties, who called a wartime truce, and of unity in the Government, which became a coalition in May 1915. And it also emphasised the need for franchise reform. The old parliamentary register was already destined for revision before the General Election schedule for 1915, but a new list of voters became increasingly necessary for two reasons. First, the postponement of that election made the old register more outdated by the day, while, secondly, there was a popular and bipartisan demand that soldiers and sailors, disqualified either by age or for other reasons at the beginning of the War, should have a vote at the end of it. Thus electoral reform became an urgent domestic issue during the War, and, thanks to the pre-War campaign, women were also included, even though there was still considerable opposition to their claim. Cabinet discussions on the subject eventually led to the Speaker's Conference on Electoral Reform in October 1916 (*ibid.*:134–150). It became increasingly untenable, and at odds with the need to maintain and encourage patriotic fervour, not to enfranchise military men (and perhaps women war workers too).

Wartime patriotism particularly affected the Tory position on franchise reform. Before the War many Tories had been opposed to women's suffrage on the grounds that it would be a further step towards universal suffrage. Yet a large number were now adamant that the soldiers and sailors should be enfranchised, partly in the hope that a fervently nationalist electorate would vote in their favour (Close 1977:899). But some Tory MPs were still privately opposed to women's suffrage, and only as it became ever more likely that women would be voting in the next election did the fear of losing these new votes make them change their position. They welcomed the age limit in the hope that older women would be more conservative – even though the next step could only be universal suffrage. Less wary of Labour after its brief term of office in 1924 and convinced of the conservative benefits of adult suffrage, Baldwin, the Tory leader, pushed through the Parliamentary Reform Act in 1928 (*ibid*.:910–18).

The War had removed other obstacles in the path of women's suffrage: now that there was a Coalition Government the Irish Nationalist opposition to votes for women was no longer important (Morgan 1975:147–8); Asquith had been replaced by the pro-suffragist Lloyd George; and the 'antis' could no longer point to the frailty of women as a reason for excluding them from the register. 'It was wildly illogical to be converted to Women's Suffrage because a girl who had been a good milliner could also be a good lift attendant,' Ray Strachey wrote, but, for some men, 'so it was' (Strachey 1928:345). This reflected a curious irony for many suffragists: they saw that the climax of the male characteristics of violence, aggression and power – war – had demolished, through women's work in the factories and the fields, the old myth that the female sex was incapable of physical force or of being involved in the defence of the nation. Nor could the 'antis' justify their view on the basis of the excesses of suffragette militancy – this was long dead.

These political and social developments meant that the opponents of women's suffrage had little chance when the Representation of the People Bill finally reached the Lords. There were rumours of a last ditch stand by the 'antis', led by Lord Curzon, but, faced with majority support for the Bill in the Commons and apparently in the country too, they were forced to capitulate. The Lords could have thrown the women's clause out but, as Curzon warned, this would only have led to another battle with the Commons and with the party to which most of the Peers belonged (Fawcett 1920:147). The Bill was passed by 134 votes to 71, with most of the leading 'antis' abstaining. According to Millicent Fawcett 'the forces of freedom and self government finally overcame the forces of autocracy' (*Cause* January 18, 1918:516). Despite the age limit, itself put in to allay 'anti' fears, the principle had been won – as well as votes for over eight million women (compared with nearly 13 million men).

Although the War was crucial to the suffragists' success, their own contribution must not be ignored. The fact that votes for women had become an integral part of the electoral reform debate was due to their pre-War campaign and, to a lesser extent, to their pressure from 1916 onwards. (The WFL even picketed the Speaker's Conference.) The suffragists had campaigned for years, while the suffragettes of the WSPU, in spite of or because of their militant tactics, had re-awakened interest in votes for women. Thus when war broke out in 1914, women's suffrage, whatever its chances of success, was still very much on the political agenda. There were signs, too, that Asquith was beginning to change his mind. How far was this due to the suffragettes? And how far was it in response to the non-militants' campaign?

The crucial problem for suffragists and suffragettes alike was to convince the Liberal Government that votes for women were a political necessity. They had to demonstrate that the Liberals ultimately had more to gain than to lose by granting women's suffrage: besides the arguments about women's roles and duties, the issue of party advantage was also important. And, by 1912, it was clear that only a government measure would do: most sections of the suffrage movement had abandoned their faith in private members' bills which had failed to progress due to lack of government facilities, and particularly of time. Thus Stranger's Bill had passed its second reading by a majority of 179 in 1908, the Conciliation Bills by 110 (in 1910) and 167 (in 1911), but they had not ultimately succeeded. The latter had been 'torpedoed' by a promise of a women's suffrage amendment to the Government's forthcoming Reform Bill which eventually was ruled out of order by the Speaker in January 1913. Asquith may well have described 'the Speaker's *coup d'état*' as 'a great relief' (Rover 1967a:196) yet the problem, as he must have realised, was not simply going to disappear.

The question posed to suffragists was how to force Asquith to change his mind. And the answer for the suffragettes was ever increasing militancy. Yet despite suffragette bravery and their willingness to die for the cause, the political strategy of their leaders was flawed in both general and specific ways. First, their militancy was individualistic – it was divorced from mass involvement. In spite of cabinet worries and individual attacks of ministers (a hatchet was thrown at Asquith in Dublin – and missed), the militancy of the suffragettes was less threatening than that of Carson, organising armed revolt in Ireland against the possibility of Home Rule, or that of the miners, dockers and transport workers. Sadly, the fact that the suffragettes were willing to risk their own lives but not endanger those of others, also made their campaign less powerful. The lack of cohesion in the militant campaign did not help either – for example, important Liberal businesses were not systematically attacked. Secondly, the more Asquith refused to budge, the more desperate militancy became, and, in turn, the more likely it was to antagonise support for suffragism: suffragette militancy was both inconvenient and embarrassing to Asquith, but, even if it did influence him, could he be seen to capitulate?

Thirdly, the Pankhursts' strategy was flawed on specific political points. Their anti-Liberal and anti-Labour stance could only benefit one party – the Tories. Yet, as Teresa Billington-Grieg noted, the Conservatives never gave a firm pledge on women's suffrage. In other words, even if the WSPU's campaign had led to the downfall of the Liberals and the establishment of a Tory Government, there was no guarantee of a women's bill. Indeed, given the strong 'anti' element within the Conservative and Unionist Party and the fears of universal suffrage, it hardly seemed likely at all. Some Unionists, for example Bonar Law, were pro-suffrage but would only envisage a limited measure (Morgan 1975:86).

And, finally, it is arguable that the renewal of suffragette militancy at the end of 1911 was damaging to their cause. Asquith had just announced his Reform Bill but the WSPU refused to accept his promise of a women's suffrage amendment and renewed their militant campaign. This scotched an apparent plan by Lloyd George to go on a national pro-suffrage campaign with other suffragist sympathisers (*ibid.*), while it probably also had an adverse effect on the Dickenson Bill of 1912. Whether or not Lloyd George would have risked the collapse of the Government over women's suffrage is open to question. But if Asquith was to change his position it could not have been on the basis of submitting to the Pankhursts. It could only have been solely on the basis of political expediency and in a manner that would not in any way harm the Liberals, and, rather, would hopefully enhance their prospect of further electoral success.

The suffragists, so long ignored in the 'bombs and chains' accounts of the struggle for the vote, come in at this point. Their strategy was crucial in moving Asquith along the road towards women's suffrage. They, too, had forsaken the private member's bill strategy by the end of 1911, but had, crucially, linked suffragism to the Labour movement and to class. This approach, which reflects the different political perspectives of the two major wings of the suffrage movement, was clearly aimed at pressurising the Liberals. The NUWSS's Election Fighting Fund, for example, aimed to increase Labour representation in the Commons while improving their constituency organisation, particularly in seats held by anti-suffragist Liberals. What evidence there is suggests that it worked: the 'Labour vote rose significantly in all but one of the by-elections in which it was employed' (Newbury 1977:412; see also Pugh 1978:23).

The link between suffragists and Labour enabled Asquith to see the problem in terms of class rather than of sex, and also in terms of party advantage: after 1910 the NUWSS were increasingly arguing that their demand was not for the propertied but for the mass of women; and after the famous Summer Pilgrimage of 1913, which confirmed the wide support for women's suffrage, Margaret Robertson emphasised to Asquith that he should see the problem 'not as a sex question but as a democratic one' (*Cause* August 15, 1913:319). Given the potential threat from Labour to the Liberals *and* the prospect of a General Election in 1915, surely Asquith, despite his own personal hostility to women's suffrage, was gradually realising that the change had to come? Perhaps he was even considering a commitment to women's votes at the election in 1915?

Certainly, the Prime Minister's response to the working class deputation from the ELFS in June 1914 seemed to indicate a change of heart. After very clearly distancing himself from the 'criminal methods' of the WSPU he made his significant statement implying that if women were to have the vote this would have to be on a wide basis (Asquith to Sylvia Pankhurst's East End Deputation June 20, 1914; quoted in *Women's Dreadnought* June 27, 1914:57). The Liberal Prime Minister, mindful of the forthcoming General Election was, as many contemporary observers realised, beginning to change his tune. Henry Nevinson, for example, argued that the deputation had 'a remarkable effect on Mr Asquith's mind' (Nevinson 1925:337), while Emmeline Pethick-Lawrence considered that it was 'the first sign that he was beginning to change his attitude of hostility to women's suffrage' (E. Pethick-Lawrence 1938:304–5). 'Beneath his words', *The Labour Leader* argued, 'there seemed to be a recognition that the enfranchisement of women cannot long be delayed' (quoted in *Women's Dreadnought* July 4, 1914:65); or, as *The Common Cause* put it, 'Mr Asquith Begins To Take Notice' (*Cause* June 26, 1914:243).

The crisis of the War ended the speculation over Asquith's attitude. Yet the suffragists had succeeded in explaining their case not only in a way that their prime political opponent could understand but in a way that allowed him to change course. Crucially, they had established votes for women within the wider context of electoral reform – the one could no longer be realistically discussed without the other. So although it cannot be denied that the suffragettes had drawn attention to the suffrage movement – by 1914 the problem of the hunger strikers was particularly acute – for all the individual bravery and ingenuity, the validity of their leaders' strategy is clearly open to question, and credit to the 'non-militants' is long overdue.

While the suffragist strategy before 1914 and the new political conditions created by the War indeed made votes for women increasingly likely, other factors are worthy of consideration too. The War, as has been described, heightened political instability and furthered militant class struggle. On the industrial front, the shop stewards' movement continued to challenge the authority of the Government and, by implication, Parliament as well. Strikes against dilution or broken workplace agreements increased: in May 1917 alone, 1½ million working days were lost due to industrial disputes. The Leeds Soviet Convention of the following month called for the creation of workers' and soldiers' councils and the success of Lenin in October encouraged revolutionaries everywhere. By the middle of 1917 it seemed as if 'the Home Front was in a state of incipient revolt' (Kendall 1969:157).

The end of the War, with the problems of demobilisaticn, reconstruction and an embittered population aware of the fact that victory against the Germans had brought little tangible reward, brought no respite. Mutinies in the armed forces spread while the Red Flag flew briefly over one of His Majesty's ships (HMS Kilbride) in 1919. The police in London, Birmingham and Liverpool even went on strike, prompting an overjoyed Sylvia Pankhurst to declare 'spirit of Petrograd! . . . After that anything may happen!' (*Workers' Dreadnought* September 7, 1918:1069). The War Office felt it necessary to send, in *The Daily Herald*'s words (May 13, 1919), 'a confidential questionnaire to the commanding officers of all units in order to ascertain whether or not it was thought that the troops would remain loyal in the case of a revolution in England' (Kendall 1969:190; 187–194).

It was in this unstable and potentially revolutionary context that promises of 'Homes Fit For Heroes' and other reforms in rent control, council housing and education were made. The revolution did not come, but the ruling class was rattled. It is not beyond the realms of possibility that the vote was granted, too, as Lord Russell implied, to stave off 'riot revolution and rifle' (House of Lords December 17, 1917). Certainly, Lord Curzon, the leading 'anti' of pre-War days, was not alone in being wary of revolution in 1917–18. The consequences of precipitating a constitutional crisis through refusing to accept the Representation of the People Bill could not be risked – even though the Bill included women's suffrage (Harrison 1978:209).

Not surprisingly, Sylvia Pankhurst thought the fear of revolution an important factor in the granting of votes to women. In November 1918, in an article entitled, 'Parliament Doomed', she observed that 'In every country Parliaments are threatened . . . Realising this the old fogeys of

Parliament, and the powers behind them are saying: "We must do something to popularise the old institution; let us bring in the Women" ' (*Workers' Dreadnought* November 2, 1918:1106). Five years later she added that 'the legal barriers to Women's participation in Parliament and its elections were not removed until the movement to abolish Parliament altogether had received the strong encouragement of witnessing the overthrow of Parliamentary Government in Russia and the setting up of Soviets' (*ibid.* December 15, 1923:1). The granting of votes to women had become increasingly likely even before the War began, but Sylvia's explanation remains plausible. Was it purely a fear of a majority female franchise or perhaps the hope that older women would be less rebellious that lay behind the 30-years age bar?

In conclusion it should be added that the granting of the vote may have been connected with the post-War problems of demobilisation and reconstruction. The Government had to cope with women who had tasted economic independence and whose jobs were now threatened by the return of the men. Agreements with trade unions and legislation such as the Pre-War Practices Act meant that women workers, unless in new or well established women's trades, had to leave once the War was over: 'The women's saga was over. One by one, the jobs in which they had been respected and rewarded vanished' (Adam 1975:72). Was the vote a sop to sweeten the bitterness of an enforced return to the old customs, to assure women of their worthiness as citizens? After the great loss of life they were indeed expected to return to their old duty as mothers of the race, hence, for example, the Maternity and Child Welfare Act of 1918. How likely would co-operation be if women, so highly praised for their contribution to the war effort and who had to accept the slaughter of their sons, were denied the elementary political right of the vote?

Thus the old analysis of the suffragists' success in 1918 is clearly inadequate. The vote was not simply given as a reward for their work during the War or to ward off the threat of renewed suffragette militancy. It was the result of a combination of factors, some more readily identifiable than others. Most importantly, the War removed some of the grounds for opposition to women's suffrage that had existed before 1914. It changed the relationship between the political parties and it removed an 'anti' Prime Minister. The Pankhursts (Christabel and Emmeline) had suspended militancy so that 'antis' could no longer use this as a reason for their opposition to votes for women. Crucially, too, the War increased the urgency of franchise reform generally and the suffragists had ensured that such reform had to include some measure for women. Many 'antis' were (or seemed to be) converted and even the Conservative Party, perhaps less uneasy given the 30-years age limit, voted for the 1918 Bill. Revolution was in the air and, if women were to remain loyal to the state, their wartime effort and sacrifice had to be acknowledged. In such a confused and fluid environment were votes for women finally won. And although to suffragists like Nina Boyle of the Women's Freedom League the passing of a Bill with a measure of votes for women, 'so long delayed, means power' (*Vote* January 25, 1918:124), the devastation of war, and to a lesser extent, the age limit, meant that it was a sad and hollow victory, an anti-climax to a long campaign.

8 Conclusion

. . . the right of women to the vote must be discussed on another basis than the value of the franchise. Their claim is to be recognised as intelligent human beings.
(Victor Grayson, *The Problem of Parliament – A Criticism and A Remedy* 1909)

The vote cannot secure of itself any single woman's emancipation . . . [suffragists] fail to see that large areas in which emancipation is needed lie entirely outside the scope of the vote . . . a slave woman with a vote will still be essentially a slave.
(Teresa Billington-Grieg, *The Militant Suffrage Movement – Emancipation in a Hurry* c.1911)

The agitation for the vote was one for a reform inside the bourgeois State. Necessary at one time, it is now very much a thing of the past.
(*Workers' Dreadnought* August 9, 1921)

'It was the greatest moment of my life. We had won fairly and squarely after a fight lasting fifty years. Henceforth, Women would be free citizens' (Fawcett 1924:247). How far was this true? How far would the vote and legislation improve the position of women? Millicent Fawcett's personal jubilation in 1918 is not difficult to understand but the passing of the Representation of The People Act, with its limited measure of votes for women, saw a sad day for suffragism too. The War had already split the movement, and the old days of demonstrations, deputations and militancy were over. Some suffragists continued to campaign in the National Union of Societies for Equal Citizenship (the old NUWSS) or the Women's Freedom League. They adopted programmes which called for equal pay, greater job opportunities and equality within the law. The WFL's manifesto was summed up in the slogan 'Full Equality in every direction of Women with Men' (*Vote* January 3, 1919). Yet the membership of both organisations shrank and the women's suffrage movement was no longer part of a struggle that involved thousands of women.

How should it now, some 60 years later, be assessed? How should its ideas be evaluated? First, on a wider historical level, it is clear that the importance of both the NUWSS and, to a lesser extent, the WFL has been under-rated. Concentration on the Pankhursts has, by implication, mistakenly resulted in the drab and boring image of the non-militants, while, at the same time, over-rating the WSPU's contribution to the actual winning of the vote. The evidence suggests that the strategies of the NUWSS and WFL were crucial to the victory of 1918. Furthermore, the feminist and political analyses of the NUWSS and the WFL became increasingly radical and increasingly associated with the demands of working class women. Ultimately this led to the introduction of the question of class into the debate on women's inequality and to a growing identification with the wider demands of the Labour movement, all of which stood in marked contrast to the autocracy and élitism of the WSPU leadership (and was perhaps responsible for the phenomenal growth of the NUWSS after 1910).

The evidence also suggests that the belief, still widely held, that the Pankhursts were political revolutionaries needs to be questioned. As Guy Aldred and Teresa Billington-Grieg argued at the time, militant tactics do not necessarily reflect a militant ideology. Indeed, in many ways, Christabel and Emmeline Pankhurst represented the most conservative components of the whole suffrage movement. It could be argued that the WSPU, abandoning its working class origins as early as 1906, moved inexorably towards the anti-socialist position of the Women's Party in 1917. Both its structure and its tactics prevented free and open debate, and, in fact by 1912, to Christabel, 'nothing matters but methods, so far as Women's Suffrage is concerned' (*Suffragette* December 13, 1912:130). As Annie Kenney recalled in her memoirs, only two questions would hold suffragette audiences 'spellbound' – history and militancy: 'Why Women wanted the vote was tame, dull, uninteresting. How Women would get it was exciting, romantic, amusing' (Kenney 1924:147).

Yet the militant campaign cannot be dismissed merely because of the views of the WSPU's leaders. Many suffragettes agreed with militancy but were forced to leave the Union, while militancy itself clearly reawakened a moribund campaign and kept it in the forefront of political debate. Moreover, it completely destroyed some prevailing notions of female characteristics. As the liberal feminist Winifred Holtby was to conclude, 'it disproved the theories about women's nature which were among their gravest handicaps. It broke down taboos . . . Women had accepted discipline, displayed capacity of organisation, courage and tenacity. The very recklessness and extremism of militancy had shaken old certainties' (Holtby 1934:52–3).

It should also be noted that militancy fed on something far more important than the inequalities of the franchise. Surely no suffragette freely offered herself to ridicule, imprisonment, torture and possibly death, just for the vote? The vote, or the lack of it, was symbolic of women's oppression and inequality, and suffragism and militancy reflected this. Certainly, suffragettes subsequently argued that their campaign was

much more than votes for women. We were inaugurating a new era for women
and demonstrating for the first time in history that women were capable of
fighting their own battle for freedom's sake. We were breaking down old
senseless barriers which had been the curse of our sex, exploding men's theories
and ideas about us.

(Richardson 1953:103)

Notwithstanding contemporary criticisms militancy was perhaps
the clearest (and most irritating) manifestation of the reaction against
women's oppression upon which suffragism was based. It challenged
'the standard of values which rated women's persons, position, interests and pre-occupations as affairs of minor national importance'
(Holtby 1934:53), and it implied an attack on the 'natural' roles of
women. Yet did suffragism direct energies from wider feminist goals –
was 'the woman . . . sacrificed to the getting of the vote' (Billington-
Grieg 1911:218)?

Certainly, tactical considerations seemed to limit wider and public
discussions of sex and contraception, and many of the feminist and
political prescriptions of suffragism may now seem limited and narrow,
but a great number of the suffragist ideas did relate directly to the
specific oppression of women. Some suffragist arguments did develop
beyond a mere call for the vote and attacked other results of the
inequality between the sexes. Many attacked the economic dependence
of women; all of them attacked the vast disparities in the law. The
majority of suffragists also defended a woman's right to work and
criticised the gulf between the ideal and the reality of motherhood and
domesticity. These 'natural' roles were even defined as work and, as
such, required payment. Here there appears to have been a contradiction between the prevailing acceptance of women's sphere and the
demands for wider opportunities, but suffragists insisted that they
wanted a choice for women.

Although the attitudes revealed towards sex and birth control may
well now seem to have been limited, they cannot be dismissed. Suffragist prescriptions on sexual morality which may appear narrow now
were understandable within their own context: given the difficulties of
obtaining economic independence from men and the concern over
venereal disease, it is hardly surprising that many women opted for the
safety of monogamous marriage. And, moreover, many suffragists
besides Mrs Pankhurst did attack the generally ambivalent and oppressive attitude of men towards women and sex, while the WFL's
'Protected Sex' series exposed the hypocrisy of the moral code (*Vote*
1913–14). By contrasting sentences passed against the violation of
private property with those passed against the violation of women, it
condemned the real values behind the law.

It has to be recognised, however, that many suffragist ideas rested on acceptance of the allegedly natural and biologically defined roles and characteristics of women. Suffragism had clearly inherited the argument that men and women had different roles and characteristics, and that until the latter were fully represented, society and government would be unbalanced. This attitude prevented a clear analysis of sex stereotypes from emerging and women's biology became confused with socially defined characteristics. Here the suffragist defence – they were calling for choice in the options open to women – does seem weak. How could all women have had this choice if their 'natural' role was, after all in the home and the family?

The suffragists' ideas have to be seen within the context of their environment. A more radical and public approach to sex, for example, would have been extremely difficult in the moral climate of the 1900s and would have been a boon to the opposition, always ready with charges of immorality. Moreover, as has been suggested (chapter 1), there were very clear social and political pressures on women to conform to their 'natural' roles. Suffragists were operating in a male world where their opponents chose both the venue and the rules of the game. This not only explains the underlying opposition to votes for women but also the nature of much of the suffragists' response – they were forced to answer on their opponent's level. Thus women had to prove that the vote would not break up the home, that it would not endanger the race nor challenge motherhood, as the 'antis' implied.

What is remarkable is that, despite these constraints, the debate within democratic suffragism widened and began to embrace criticisms of the predominant assumptions about women. And women as a group across class boundaries could identify with the arguments of the suffrage movement. However, given its ideological inheritance, it is not surprising that many of the movement's arguments rested on the sexual division of labour and on an acceptance of male/female roles. This was not necessarily due to a lack of imagination but was clearly a product of the times.

However, some women did become increasingly critical of the feminist and political limitations of mainstream suffragism. Lily Gair Wilkinson (c.1910; 1914) and Rose Witcop (see Aldred 1956), for example, were critical of the suffragists' apparent obsession with the vote, and Teresa Billington-Grieg argued that it limited wider feminist perspectives from emerging (c.1911). Most of the contributors to *The Freewoman* seem to have agreed, and the debate within its pages showed, in particular, how the suffragists' emphasis on the vote appeared to restrict both their analysis of the origins of women's oppression and their prescriptions for change. *The Freewoman* discussion also suggested that the oppression of women could not be traced merely to their 'votelessness' nor could it be remedied by female suffrage. Consequently, the paper began to analyse, for example, the relationship between women's domestic and maternal roles and their inequality. This in turn led to a condemnation of proposals for wages for housework since they would merely confirm women in a role which was instrumental in maintaining their unequal status. Thus, too, came the paper's demands for state-run nurseries and the sharing of childcare between the sexes.

What many of the contributors to *The Freewoman* clearly wanted was a whole new world for women, free from contemporary definitions of their roles and capabilities. And this included sex and reproduction. *The Freewoman* emphasised the necessity of women's control of reproduction and, at the same time, demanded an end to their passive sexuality. Women like Stella Browne were attacking the whole sexual structure, not demanding reform: they wanted women to enjoy their sexuality free from the fear of pregnancy, free from the control of men. Such a position in 1911 was beset with difficulties (not least the displeasure of the distributors of the journal), and it stood in marked contrast to the aims of suffragism.

How this was to be achieved was not made clear although the general consensus was that the economic independence of women was a vital prerequisite – and that this was unlikely to be gained under capitalism. Some considered that the liberation of women was unlikely within a social system based on marriage and the family, and argued for new relationships between the sexes as well as economic equality and independence. Certainly, the majority seem to have agreed that the vote and legislation alone would not ensure the liberation of women. *The Freewoman* may not have lasted long but it did indicate some of the feminist and political limitations of mainstream suffragism while showing that contemporary feminism was wider than the struggle for the vote. In the end, *The Freewoman* represented not only a criticism of suffragism but a growing revolutionary feminism that was shunned by leading suffragists. It was a feminism which lay behind the worst fears of the 'antis'.

The political limitations of suffragist analysis were perhaps most clearly presented by Sylvia Pankhurst's organisations. Originating in the context of work in the East End, and aided by the sharpening inequality caused by the War, her revolutionary socialist position developed well beyond the political boundaries of orthodox suffragism. Though committed to the vote until 1917, the WFS ultimately called attention to the wider inequalities of capitalism and questioned the ability of legislation to remove them. Indeed, it finally argued that Parliament itself was only part of the superstructure of capitalism and that it had, in effect, little relevance to working class women and the struggle for a wider economic and social equality.

Notwithstanding the importance of its relief work for women, how-

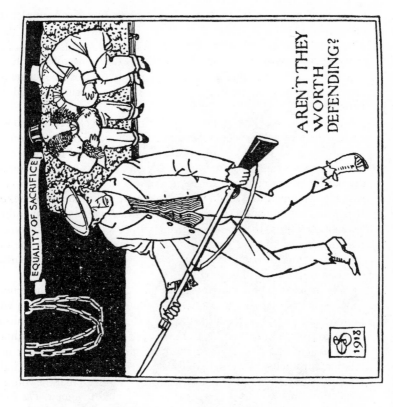

EQUALITY OF SACRIFICE

ARENT THEY WORTH DEFENDING?

1918

"HANDS OFF THE RING."

Principal Scene in the GRAND CHRISTMAS PANTOMIME — European Theatre
Continuous performance — Prices as usual.

The WSF's attitude to the war as portrayed by Herbert Cole (left) and Sylvia Pankhurst (right) in 1916 and 1918

*Countess Markievicz, the first woman to be elected to Parliament.
By courtesy of the Director and Board of Governors of the Museum
of London*

ever, the Federation's own feminism began to be submerged in the development of a revolutionary socialist position. It became a feminism that could be reduced to an economic level and one in which the specific oppression of women was lost and explained only in terms of their membership of the working class. In spite of the later discussions of some of Kollantai's work, the relationship of women's role to their oppression and to the power of men over women was neither analysed nor explained. Paradoxically, this limitation mirrored a major limitation of some of the main ideological currents within suffragism. But Sylvia Pankhurst's organisations indicated that the economic and social inequalities that working class women faced required a far wider political change than that apparently proposed by suffragism.

Finally, although the influence of both *The Freewoman* and Sylvia Pankhurst's organisations together never matched that of the women's suffrage movement, they did at least indicate the limitations of suffragism. They implied that, while suffragists were striving for formal political equality, their demands on the whole left social, economic and sexual structures intact and kept working women restricted by class and all women restricted by the domestic and maternal ideology. They posed strategic and theoretical problems for feminists too: How could the ideas of *The Freewoman*, as Mary Gawthorpe wondered (Mary Gawthorpe to Dora Marsden June 1, 1911), be infused into a wider political movement for women? How could working class women, potentially the greatest threat to capitalism and male power, be mobilised without ignoring their specific oppression as women too?

On the surface suffragism appeared to be successful in 1918. Nina Boyle, of the Women's Freedom League, could claim that for women 'there is no question we can not dominate if we so choose' (*Vote* January 25, 1918:124). But it was a shallow victory which hardly heralded a new sororial world. Not only did sexist values continue to predominate, but class and political differences between women remained unaltered. Of the 17 women who stood for Parliament in 1918, one was an Independent Unionist, one for the Coalition (Christabel Pankhurst), two for Sinn Fein, five Independent, four Liberal and four Labour – including Mary McArthur, Emmeline Pethick-Lawrence and Charlotte Despard (*Vote* January 3, 1919). There could not have been a wider gulf between the sisters, Sylvia and Christabel Pankhurst; there was a vast difference between the Irish revolutionary, Countess Markievicz, the first woman to be elected to Parliament, and the Tory, Nancy Astor, the first to actually take her seat. (Markievicz was in Holloway prison for her Republican activities when she was elected as a Sinn Feiner.) Clearly the old 'anti' fear of domination by women as a sex was groundless:

their enfranchisement did little to remove the political and class differences amongst them.

However, suffragists could claim that the vote had an immediate impact and, indeed, during the whole interwar period. Millicent Fawcett in 'What The Vote Has Done' (NUSEC October 1927) considered that the passage of seven Acts between 1918 and 1919 was directly attributable to the suffragist victory. This legislation included improvement in the laws concerning illegitimacy, midwifery and nursing. It also included the Sex Disqualification (Removal) Act of 1919 which intended to remove obstacles in the way of women who wanted to hold public office or civil and judicial posts. She argued that, throughout the 1920s, the vote had achieved what suffragists claimed – favourable legislation for women: there were Acts on Married Women's Property, Maintenance Orders, Infanticide (all 1920), Maintenance (1922), Divorce (1923), Guardianship of Infants and Pensions (both 1925). Some of these had been promoted by the National Union of Societies for Equal Citizenship (NUSEC) and they were clearly aimed at improving women's lot.

Many suffragists, with the occasional misgiving and with the proviso that much still needed to be done, certainly felt their struggle and the victories of 1918 and 1928 had been worthwhile. In *Our Freedom and Its Results* written by five suffragists in the 1930s (R. Strachey (ed.) 1936), Eleanor Rathbone claimed that 'generally, the results exceed expectations' (*ibid.*:20). She referred to the legislation outlined above, the number of women MPs (although few had her suffragist background) and the increased number of women on bodies such as Royal Commissions. Writing of the various Acts in particular, Rathbone concluded that 'this fine harvest of legislation affecting women's status and special interests, which marked the first decade since our enfranchisement, gives us old suffragists no reason to feel disillusioned' (*ibid.*:51).

Much of the legislation was indeed valuable and of direct benefit to specific groups of women. For example the Matrimonial Causes Act of 1923, promoted by NUSEC, made it possible for women to sue for divorce on the grounds of adultery on the same terms as men. The Maternity and Child Welfare Act (1918), welcomed in particular by the Women's Co-operative Guild, set up welfare clinics for mothers and babies. Yet this last Act was also passed to encourage women to replace the lives and labour lost during the War (Rowbotham 1977a:120).

Indeed, much of the legislation reflected an attitude towards women which saw them in terms of mothers, wives or widows. This in turn shows the continuing currency of the 'anti' notion of women's role and was, perhaps, part of the suffragist post-War legacy. Certainly, when the War ended the old sexual division of labour re-established itself. With few exceptions, the post-War world slid back into a clear division of jobs for men or women, and the notion that women's work outside the home was unusual, and secondary to that of men, returned. Women teachers, for example, had to resign on marriage while the pressure on women workers increased as the depression developed – married women workers were struck off the unemployment register: 'the state of the economy made it essential that women should go back home and stay there' (Adam 1975:125).

The rise of domestic consumerism in the 1930s also encouraged women's domestic role. This was reflected in the growth of women's pages in the press and a whole new range of magazines such as *Ideal Home*, *My Home* and *Wife and Mother*. These all carried clear messages about the true concerns of women (*ibid.*:127). Thus while the interwar period saw much legislation directed at women, the old definitions of their interests and capabilities had not changed. As Eleanor Rathbone argued 'progress has been rapid when it depended on political action and slow when it depended on heart and habits. What else would you expect when the instrument was the vote?' (Strachey (ed.) 1936:20). Perhaps the 'antis' had lost a battle, but not the war.

There were, arguably, some improvements in the 1920s and 1930s. There were more opportunities in office work and light industry, especially in the South of England even though the old divisions between male and female jobs remained. Attitudes towards sex may well have relaxed, but the condemnation of Radclyffe Hall's *Well of Loneliness* (1928), a novel concerning lesbianism, showed how little attitudes had really changed. 'I would rather give a healthy boy or a healthy girl a phial of prussic acid than this novel,' commented the male critic of *The Sunday Express* (Adam 1975:95). There were, however, thanks to the work of pioneers like Marie Stopes, improvements in the quality and availability of contraception, and the Abortion Law Reform Association was set up in 1936. Yet 'sexual emancipation in the 1920s and 1930s remained confined to a narrow, privileged section of society' (Rowbotham 1977a:142) – the freedom of the 'flappers' was restricted to the young, fashionable and middle class woman. Women may have had the vote but in many ways little had changed.

Feminism survived in the interwar period although no mass campaign on the scale of that surrounding the struggle for the vote emerged. This failure was due to a variety of factors, among them the legacy of suffragism itself. Although suffragism had indeed appeared to dominate the women's movement, the vote had not been the only concern of pre-War feminism, and a commitment to legislation and reform remained after the War. However, activists split up into campaigns on different issues – the unity surrounding the single demand for the vote disappeared once it had been won, and women, to the surprise of the most extreme 'antis', went their own, and often conflicting, ways.

The War had already emphasised divisions within English feminism, and these were perhaps confirmed after 1918. Revolutionary feminism subsided, in spite of the efforts of women like Stella Browne, while women in the Labour Party became engulfed in its growing reformism (Rowbotham 1977a:159–169). Feminism became even more fragmented with the launch of separate campaigns and organisations such as NUSEC, the Six Point Group and the London National Society for Women's Service, later the Fawcett Society (Doughan 1980:7). As Sylvia Pankhurst reflected in 1924, it became clearer than ever that 'the struggle to secure a fundamental change is more difficult than to obtain some slight adjustment that makes little or no challenge to vested interests . . . The problem is how to obtain for the fundamental movement the necessary momentum' (*Workers' Dreadnought* April 19, 1924:2).

The momentum behind the pre-War women's movement was clearly lost and feminism itself seemed to have little attraction for the new post-War generation of women. The older feminists writing in *Our Freedom and Its Results* appeared to feel isolated and were not uncritical of their younger sisters' apparent lack of interest. Ray Strachey complained that they showed 'a strong hostility to the word "feminism" and all which they imagine it to connote' (Strachey (ed.) 1936:9). Mary Hamilton (who had become a Labour MP) felt that they should be more grateful to the pre-War pioneers: 'those who fought for the emancipation of their sex and won it, look at the girl of today with a disappointment in which there is more than a hint of bitterness', and complained that young women were 'not interested in the status of their sex as a sex' (*ibid.*:239).

The weakening of a feminist movement was also connected with the objective conditions of the interwar period. The disillusionment of 1918 and 1919 gave way to the unemployment of the 1920s and 1930s and to the international conflicts that were to result in another war. With unemployment and the rise of fascism both at home and abroad even radical political women may have felt that 'a specific consciousness as women was a kind of indulgence' (Rowbotham 1977a:163). Winifred Holtby noted how several factors acted against feminism. She argued that there was a revival of the 'Kinder, Kuche, Kirche' philosophy while 'the economic slump . . . the resurgence of military values [and] the cult of the cradle' were responsible for forcing 'the pendulum of emancipation to swing backwards' (Holtby 1934:174).

The obstacles to the development of feminism in the interwar period prevented a return to the vitality of the 1900s and thus made the exploitation of a woman's contribution to the Second World War impossible. Once again, the old myths about women's capabilities and sphere were forgotten as they were first encouraged, then conscripted into the war effort. Yet when the Second World War was over, the wartime nurseries were shut, women's jobs vanished and they became wives and mothers again. Although the beginnings of the Welfare State brought many improvements, the thought behind the reforms was often based on a confirmation of women's domestic and maternal roles. Sir William Beveridge, the architect of the modern Welfare State, argued, for example, that

the attitude of the housewife to gainful employment outside the home is not and should not be the same as the single woman. She has other duties . . . In the next thirty years housewives and mothers have vital work to do in ensuring the adequate continuance of the British race and of British ideals in the world.

(*The Beveridge Report* 1942; quoted in Sharpe 1976:37)

Meanwhile, the view of John Bowlby, who argued that it was psychologically dangerous for mothers to leave their infants, gained currency. As Margaret Mead observed, Bowlby's theory of 'maternal deprivation' marked 'a new and subtle form of anti-feminism' (Adam 1975:166).

Nonetheless, the boom in the economy in the 1950s did provide more demand for women's labour, and by the early 1960s over half of married women were working outside the home. On the surface, the 1960s, too, brought progress in the availability of contraception and, with the 1967 Act, accessibility to safe, legal abortions. More recently still, the Equal Pay Act (1970), the Employment Protection Act (1975) and the Sex Discrimination Act (1975) mark the zenith of reform and represent a progress that would have been beyond the wildest dreams of the suffragist pioneers. They would have welcomed the Equal Opportunities Commission and would have been amazed that the law (since 1975) clearly states that it is 'unlawful to treat anyone on the grounds of sex less favourably than a person of the opposite sex is or would be treated in the same circumstances' (Equal Opportunities Commission 1977).

Thus a major suffragist assumption – that the equality of the sexes can be achieved through reform and legislation – appears to have been justified in recent years. It confirms a popular idea that there has been a linear progression towards emancipation beginning with the suffrage struggle and ending with the legislation of the 1970s. But unfortunately, this idea is demonstrably mistaken. The legislation itself is either flawed (the implementation of the Equal Pay Act, for example, took five years, giving employers enough time to organise evasion) or has had little effect. At work, women are still in the lowest paid jobs and at the bottom of most career structures. There is still a division between men's and women's work while little progress has been made towards equal pay. Few women become MPs, few have top posts within the Labour movement (Equal Opportunities Commission 1977; Toynbee 1978b; Philips 1980).

Anna Coote and Bea Campbell have revealed the failure of legislation with crystal clarity in their *Sweet Freedom – The Struggle For Women's Liberation* (1982). They record, for example, the high failure rate of applications made under the Equal Pay and the Sex Discrimination Acts. They show, too, that, on average, women's earnings in the 1970s have remained at just less than two-thirds those of men. And they illustrate how women have made little progress even in trade unions with a high female membership: in November 1980, for example, 66 per cent of NUT members were women but only four (out of a total of 44) were on the Executive Committee. It is a picture distressingly common throughout the whole trade union movement (*ibid.* 78; 140;167).

Why, despite the reforms of the last decade, has progress especially in the area of work, been so slow? The inadequacies of the legislation itself are important, but other crucial factors must be considered. In particular, the reforms do not alter women's 'natural' role and if their function remains within the family, the development of opportunities outside the home is bound to be slow. Even the Equal Opportunities Commission realised this in its report on *Women and Low Incomes* (1977):

Though outdated by reality the 'Women's place is in the home' set of attitudes remains the predominant influence on patterns of economic discrimination . . . The aim of equality, and the freeing of women from low income and poverty, cannot be achieved so long as it is women who have to bear the main burdens of looking after homes and children and caring for dependents generally.

Indeed, as Ann Oakley argued in 'The Failure of the Movement for Women's Equality' (*New Society* August 23, 1979), the reforms of the 1970s 'only scratched the surface of women's unequal treatment' as they did 'not alter the responsibilities women have for domestic work and childrearing . . . No legislation for equality can be effective if it fails to tackle the question of the relationship between "natural" sex differences and the social and domestic roles of the two genders' (*ibid.*).

This the early twentieth-century suffrage movement had failed to do.

In the final analysis it appears that suffragism had a limited concept of equality based on entry into the male world. It could well be that 'male dominance assures that the standards of humanity and social participation to which women aspire during periods of feminist rebellion are those of men' (*ibid.*). One encouraging sign today is that many feminists are rejecting such standards and would share Caroline Boord's desire for 'no ready sphere . . . [but] the whole round earth to choose from' (*Freewoman* December 14, 1911:70). However, care must be taken not to 'blame' the suffragists, nor to consider them outside the context of their own time with its unique pressures and emphases on specific male and female roles. It should be remembered that the whole suffragist rebellion reflected the oppression of women, however limited some of its prescriptions may now appear. Besides, women like Ada Nield Chew and many of the contributors to *The Freewoman* did begin to examine the effect of women's role. Moreover, some useful legislation has been passed even though 'there are limits to the kind of change which can be affected by law while the structure of society remains the same' (Rowbotham 1977a:121).

By organising as women, and by reflecting the oppression of women, perhaps suffragists were, after all, taking the first stepping stones to liberty, even though the vote may have diverted them from a wider vision of emancipation. Subsequent developments have surely shown that without change in economic and sexual structures, reform and legislation are incapable of achieving equality and liberation for women or for men. The problem is clearly more complex and must surely involve an explanation of the relationship between women, capitalism and the power of men.

Nonetheless, two factors have become clear since the suffragists' victory: first, even a limited vision of 'equality' is unlikely without changes in women's sphere; and secondly, their role is not naturally or divinely fixed but has fluctuated according to the demands of the state and of capitalism. Mother . . . war worker . . . consumer . . . and now, in the 1980s, the pressure is for women to return to the home and family to 'cure' unemployment and to fill the gaps created by the steady destruction of the Welfare State. Thus any prescription for change must isolate and explain these factors and determine their causes. At the same time, although it is particularly difficult to envisage liberation within an economic system which is based on economic inequality, the dangers of a rigid Marxist analysis cannot be ignored. The pervasive power of men has to be explained (and destroyed), too.

Liberation is an enormous task that requires more than political reform. As Dora Marsden argued in 1911, 'the great change which the Feminist Movement seeks to bring about is not merely a matter of political readjustment . . . carried to success, it would accomplish a vast revolution in the entire field of human affairs, intellectual, sexual, domestic, economic, legal and political' (*Evening Standard and St James Gazette* October 25, 1911). ' 'Tis a long row to hoe' (Ada Nield Chew, *Freewoman* April 18, 1912:436).

Appendices

I The Women's Charter of Rights and Liberties (1910)

The Women's Charter by Lady McLaren is a remarkable document which reflects the contemporary concern over the unequal position of women, both in law and in relation to men, especially to their husbands. It was published in a pamphlet which, in addition to listing the points below, included a discussion on each point in turn. Lady McLaren was a Liberal suffragist and her husband, Sir Charles McLaren, a Liberal MP. He was a keen supporter of women's suffrage and even introduced nine Parliamentary Bills based on the Charter (*Vote* April 9, 1910). These failed but aroused considerable interest; many of the proposals have been subsequently implemented. Some aspects of the Charter were startlingly radical, especially 3 (which essentially means wages for housework) and 15(b). Others reflect an acceptance of woman's sphere and duties – 15(f) – or the need for 'national efficiency' in order to compete with Germany. Nonetheless if the Charter had become law this would have represented a significant victory for women; and, at the very least, the Women's Charter reflects the breadth of the debate which suffragism inspired.

The Women's Charter of Rights and Liberties
Lady McLaren, 1910.

1 Coverture.

The whole doctrine of Coverture shall be declared obsolete and abolished by Act of Parliament.

2 Right of Maintenance.

As the law admits a wife's claim to maintenance by her husband, any wife living with her husband and not so maintained shall be able to recover a suitable maintenance by direct application to the magistrate, without intervention of the Poor Law Guardians, and such magistrate if he is satisfied that the husband can, but does not, support his wife and children, shall be empowered to make an order upon him for such a sum as he may consider suitable, and if necessary make such sum recoverable from any master who employs the husband out of wages due.

3 Earnings.

(a) A wife who devotes her whole time to housekeeping and the care of the children shall have a claim upon her husband during his life, and upon his estate after his death, for a sum calculated on a scale not exceeding the wages of a housekeeper in her station of life, provided she has not received any other personal allowance. Such sum shall not however exceed one half the amount saved during the marriage.

(b) A wife shall be a creditor for the amount on her husband's estate in case of his bankruptcy.

(c) In any dissolution of the marriage or any separation, a wife shall be entitled to payment for past services on this scale, should such payment not have been made during the marriage.

(d) Where the wife is a wage-earner she shall not be legally liable for the support of her husband or of his children, unless her earnings or the income of her property exceed the minimum necessary for her support.

(e) No wife shall be detained in the workhouse at the pleasure of her husband, if she is able and willing to support herself.

(f) No widow shall by law be obliged to maintain her children if the father's estate is sufficient for that purpose.

4 The Wife as Partner.

In any case where the husband and wife work jointly at the same business, the profits, after paying fair interest on the capital of either party, shall be regarded as joint property of the husband and wife, unless agreed otherwise by contract in writing between the parties.

5 Marriage Contracts.

Where both husband and wife possess property, marriage contracts shall be drawn up by which each party binds his or herself to make a fixed minimum contribution to house-keeping, which sum shall be recoverable by law by either party, so long as he or she shall perform the duties of the marriage. No husband or wife shall be legally liable for the expenses of the other beyond the sum agreed upon.

6 Assaults on Wives.

Magistrates shall inflict heavier penalties on men convicted of brutality to women and especially to wives. Wives and children of men so convicted and sent to prison, shall be entitled to support, but not as paupers, during the term of the husband's sentence, by a rate levied directly on the locality where they live.

7 Divorce.

The law of Divorce shall be amended as follows:

(a) To entitle either party to a divorce on the ground of unfaithfulness alone.

(b) To allow either party to obtain a dissolution of marriage on any of the following grounds: habitual drunkenness, lunacy, and cruelty.

(c) Where husband or wife after desertion has left the country, power to be given to effect service of citation by publication in the *London Gazette* (as in bankruptcy) without requiring personal services to be effected outside Great Britain.

(d) To allow a marriage to be dissolved in this country on any of these grounds by the petition of a wife where the husband is a foreigner, thus relieving the wife of the difficulty of applying to foreign Courts of Law.

(e) The Court of First Instance for the consideration of Matrimonial Causes to be the County Court of the district in which parties have resided during the greater part of the year preceding the presentation of the petition for Divorce, Judicial Separation, or Nullity of Marriage. The facts upon which the petition is based to be verified by affidavit, and be subject to cross-examination which shall take place in camera, except on the motion for judgement. All appeals to be to the Judges of the Divorce Division of the High Court, who shall be the Appellate Court for all matrimonial causes.

8 Children.

(a) Fathers and mothers shall be joint guardians of their children. In case of difference of opinion the Court on an originating summons shall decide in accordance with what it considers to be the benefit of the child.

(b) The mother shall be recognised as a parent for the purposes of the Vaccination Act.

(c) In case of the death of a first illegitimate child, due to the violence or neglect of the mother within a month of the child's birth, the penalty imposed shall be not more than two years' imprisonment, to be followed by a period of two years' industrial training.

(d) Children born to parents before marriage shall be legitimised by subsequent marriage.

(e) Illegitimate children shall succeed in cases of intestacy to real and personal property by maternal descent or through paternal descent on proof of formal adoption.

9 Domicile.

The law of England shall be assimilated in this respect to that of Germany, namely, that no woman can be bound to accept a foreign domicile against her will.

10 Marriage Service.

The House of Commons shall request the Bishops of the Church of England in Convocation to draw up a new marriage service in accordance both with womanly dignity and with legal truth.

11 Inheritance.

(a) The ancient right of wives to dower shall be restored, shall be extended to personalty, and shall be made independent of the husband's disposition, whether by deed or will.

(b) In cases of intestacy of either husband or wife the respective rights of husband, wife and children to real property shall be the same as in the case of personal property.

(c) In case of the husband or wife dying intestate, leaving a survivor of the marriage, the widow or widower so surviving shall take half the real and personal estate, and the remaining half shall be divided equally between the children.

(d) Where there are no children the surviving husband or wife shall inherit the whole property.

(e) Mothers shall inherit from children equally with fathers.

12 Testamentary Power.

No person shall have power to disinherit his or her children, and testamentary power shall extend to not more than half the property of either parent. After providing for the payment of dower the other half shall be divided in equal shares between the children of the marriage.

13 Education of Girls.

(a) The amount of money spent on each girl per head in Elementary Schools shall be equal to that expended on each boy.

(b) A sum equal to that expended on boys shall be placed at the disposal of every Education Authority for the Secondary Education of Girls.

(c) An enquiry shall be instituted into all the funds bequeathed for purposes of education, and an equal share shall be given to each sex in consideration of the past misappropriation of funds left for the education of girls.

(d) In view of the urgent need of technical education for women, every facility and inducement given to boys to obtain such education shall be extended also to girls.

(e) All Universities, Colleges, Societies, Inns of Court, institutes and public bodies, deriving money or authority from the State shall open their advantages equally to men and women.

14 Immorality.

(a) The age at which a girl can legally consent to her own dishonour shall be raised to 18 years, and that legal marriage should not be permitted before that age.

(b) The government shall appoint a commission of women to consider the best means of stamping out open immorality and carrying out the existing laws to suppress disorderly houses.

15 Measures for Improving the Condition of Married Women of the Working Classes.

(a) Parliament shall make a provision for the education and appointment of qualified midwives to replace the women driven from practice by recent legislation.

(b) Parliament shall compel municipalities to establish creches and playrooms for the working class children, on the model of the German Pestalozzi Froebel House.

(c) Parliament shall compel municipalities in large towns to provide milk suitable for the food of infants and young children.

(d) Parliament shall compel municipalities to establish cheap eating-houses and kitchens in working class centres, on the model of those established in Berlin.

(e) Parliament shall compel municipalities to establish wash-houses appropriate to the needs of the community in working class or crowded localities.

(f) Schools shall be established in large centres where instruction in all branches of the domestic arts shall be given to women and girls at low charges.

16 Factory Acts and Economics.

(a) In every case where the law forbids the mother to continue her occupation before or after the birth of her child, the legislature shall make the local authority responsible for her support during the time of prohibition, whether it can recover such charges from the husband or not.

(b) All regulations as to work and overtime which apply to women shall be extended, wherever applicable, to men working at the same trade.

(c) A distinction shall be made between the labour of young persons of both sexes, and that of adult persons, and adult women shall be allowed in certain trades to engage in night-work, provided the hours of employment are not excessive. An adult person shall mean any person over 25 years of age.

(d) Parliament shall provide greater facilities for relaxing the rigid action of the Factory Acts in certain trades where adult women are employed, either by allowing overtime or permitting a system of shifts by which the working day is prolonged at certain seasons.

(e) The attention of the legislature shall be called to the fact of the exclusion of women from many skilled trades by the action of the men's Trade Unions, and enactments shall be passed giving special facilities for the education of women in these trades and freedom to engage in them.

(f) Every effort shall be made to induce Parliament to raise the wages of women, not only by providing for them an industrial training, but by opening to them more branches of the public service.

(g) Equal payment to women and men for equal services shall be the rule in the Government offices.

(h) No local Education authority shall dismiss female school teachers merely on the ground of marriage, but these shall be permitted to continue their work as long as they are capable of effectively performing their duties as teachers.

(i) Women Factory Inspectors shall be appointed in fair proportion to the number of women workers.

(j) Authority for regulations affecting the employment of women shall be transferred from the Home Office to the Board of Trade.

17 Political Rights.

(a) The right to vote at all municipal and local elections, together with the power to serve on local bodies, shall be accorded to women equally and on the same terms with men.

(b) No woman otherwise qualified shall be excluded by sex or marriage from exercising the Parliamentary Franchise.

II The Freewoman *and Suffragism*

The political and feminist limitations of mainstream suffragism were, as described in chapter 5, outlined in the debate within *The Freewoman*. Pertinent though the paper's criticisms were, women like Ada Nield Chew chided the editors for their virulent attacks on suffragism. They felt that the struggle for the vote could not be easily dismissed, whereas Dora Marsden, who very probably wrote both the articles reprinted below, felt that its limited aim reflected the limits of the movement's leaders.

In the first article, 'Suffragism', Dora Marsden criticised the radical American, Upton Sinclair. She considered naive his call (in his 'Impressions of English Suffragism', *Freewoman* July 4, 1912:125) for suffragette leaders to organise, in conjunction with militants in the Labour movement, a general strike until their demands were met. (Not surprisingly, the Pankhursts rejected Sinclair's idea.) Dora Marsden argued that such a policy was unlikely as, to her, most suffragist leaders lived off the spoils of capitalism, and that their conservatism led them to defend current codes of morality and the institution of marriage. Thus, free and radical debate within the suffrage movement was stifled.

M. P. Willcocks, however, disagreed and, in her letter included in the second article, 'Ideas, or no Ideas?', criticised the sweeping generalisations of the first. She reminded the editor that suffragists had many varying opinions while many Northern working women were among the keenest supporters of the struggle for the vote. Moreover, the NUWSS had just developed 'a fighting policy' with Labour.

Dora Marsden stressed that the major suffragist organisations still stifled discussion within their ranks: the WSPU substituted militancy for thought; the WFL was riddled with autocracy; and the NUWSS could be represented (or misrepresented) by the views of one woman, Agnes Maude Royden. All in all, Dora concluded, suffragists were 'safer without a programme. To want a vote, and want it now, is a small affair, but it has the merit of sincerity.'

TOPICS OF THE WEEK.

Suffragism.

IT is perhaps natural that detached impressions
of the disturbances arising out of the unsettling
of traditional opinion regarding women in England
should give visitors to this country the idea that
revolutionary thought would have a natural appeal
to Englishwomen. That what would appear to be
the most advanced section of the female rebellion
should be unprepared even to give a hearing to outside suggestion is calculated therefore to give a shock
to the visitor who thinks he has tumbled across a
situation of vast possibilities. To those who have
watched the " movement " for any length of time in
England, however, the shock is, that any should have
considered it credible that a development in a pure
suffrage policy could be possible. Its limitations
have so effectively been advanced as safeguards and
advantages that it is small wonder a programme
suggesting that the limitations—the pillars of the
movement—be removed should have met with the
reception which Mr. Sinclair's has. The women's
suffrage movement in England will doubtless be
written of as the " Idealess " movement. There are
ideas in England, but there is no idea behind
English suffragism. The Suffragists—less and
more—want the vote, and they would like it now.
Why? No reason, except that men have it.
Suffragists *have* no reasons, apart from the one
given above. They make up a few to suit particular
audiences as they go along. In their official
capacity Suffragists are devoid of all social,
political, or religious philosophy. For evidence,
one may read their literature. For proof, one must
talk to them. And the more rebellious the rebels
are, the more this holds true. There is no feminism
in suffragism, nor is there any penetrating
humanism. This explains why they have put forward no programme of demands. They have
nothing to put forward specifically as their own.
Suffragists think that women are badly paid, and
they think that prostitution is wrong. But they think
these things from the *outside*, not from the inside.
There are few badly paid women in the suffrage
organisations, and there are fewer prostitutes.
Nor is there any really vital impulse towards
suffragism among the better-paid women Trade
Unionists. Suffragism is inspired and carried on, on the
one hand, by professional women, and, on the other,
by well-to-do independent women. And in this position the suffrage movement hangs fire. It appears
incapable of moving in any direction. It cannot
take up the economic line, because its chief pro-
moters live on the spoils of the system which they
would have to break up. If the women who pay
for the agitation being engineered as it is at present,
were asked to declare how many of them actually
lived on the Rent, Interest, or Profit, which account
for the suffering through poverty of the workers,
and who support the movement out of these,
it would become quite clear why there could
emerge no people's movement from the suffrage
ranks. If it became clear that the suffrage
movement had any connection with economic
justice, that it would lead to a repudiation of
the rights of Rent, Interest, and Profit, there would
be a grand trek outwards! In the same way,
there can be no whole-hearted assault upon the
disease of prostitution. Just as they stand to defend
the Capitalist monopoly, they stand to defend the
marriage monopoly. They neither want freedom,
nor will they accord it. They must preserve the
marriage-bond, because—*precisely because*—should

they destroy it, they would fear to trust to the bond
of attraction. Therefore, bind the unwilling
partner. What attraction fails to effect, the penal
code will bring about. So, too, with the prostitute.
To Suffragists, the prostitute is a figure of speech.
She is the climax of the suffrage oration. She is
the successful bait. Oratory which has failed thus
far will succeed here. The real temper of
suffragism towards the prostitute is to be gauged a
little higher up the scale—before she has arrived,
so to speak. As is usual, tribute only becomes hers
when she has achieved success : become the real
thing—in a lock hospital, for preference, and for
oratory. When first she tries her luck outside the
marriage monopoly is the time to see how she is
treated. Steps she never so little aside, for love and
not for wages, they treat her as blackleg labour
should be treated. Should she be one of the Usurer
Class, drawing her toll of interest from the toil of
others, able to live without labouring in return, their
heaviest sentence is outlawry—they make her a
social pariah. At this stage they have no use for
her on their platforms ; they would not welcome her
in their processions. She is not the finished product ; unlike the free-lance who works for what she
eats, she fails to win tribute from them to the last.
Her sister, who works, has more to look forward
to. Hunted from post to post, she begins to sell
what before she was rash enough to give, and from
this point all the possibilities of last honours are
hers. She may not know it, but tears of exquisite
sympathy will flow from eyes of good women stirred
by sonorous periods.

All things considered, therefore, Suffragists are
safer without a programme. " To want the vote,
and want it now," is a small affair, but it has the
merit of sincerity.

THE
FREEWOMAN

A WEEKLY HUMANIST REVIEW

No. 34. Vol. II.   THURSDAY, JULY 11, 1912   THREEPENCE

[Registered at G.P.O.
As a Newspaper.]

Editor:
DORA MARSDEN, B.A.

CONTENTS

IDEAS, OR NO IDEAS?

MISS M. P. WILLCOCKS writes: "It is not without ironic significance that the first article in THE FREEWOMAN of July 4th on "Justice" should be followed by one on "Suffragism," which may act as a startling object-lesson on the fallibility of human justice as expounded in a paper supposed to be on the side of freedom. For the gist of the second article is that Suffragists are contemptible, because, as a body, they have neither refused to live on Rent, Profit, or Interest, nor repudiated the institution of marriage. Women are, therefore, not to be enfranchised unless they first declare themselves to be Socialists and Free-lovers, that is, unless they subscribe to the particular creed of the Editor of THE FREEWOMAN. And this is justice in its newest aspect! I submit that it differs in no respect from the ideas of freedom and justice expressed by those Conservatives who would give the vote to women could it be proved that all women were of that particular party. It is further stated in this article that there is no programme of Suffragism. Officially there is not. And naturally so, since Suffragists are reformers of all schools of thought whose common meeting-ground is that they believe in the political equality of men and women, to the attainment of which the first step is the vote. Personally, I myself, like most other Suffragists, could supply THE FREEWOMAN with my own programme of demands which I intend my vote to help. And that is all which should be asked of a Suffragist. I myself, again, should also agree with the Editor's condemnation of living by Profit, Rent, or Interest, or by marriage, which latter, when childless and idle, is, in my opinion, nothing but prostitution under State patronage; but I should no more think of impressing my particular creed on my fellow-women as a sine quâ non to their being enfranchised than I

should of subscribing to the tenets of the Inquisition.

As to there being no impulse towards Suffragism among the better-paid women Trade Unionists, it is well known to all who are working for the cause that there are no keener Suffragists than the women textile workers of the North—who are mostly Trade Unionists. Nor is it any slur on Suffragism to say that it is upheld largely by professional and "independent" women, for the first have education, knowledge of the workaday world, and a certain certificate of efficiency given by their professional standing, while the second, by the very fact of their belonging to the movement, have proved that they can o'erleap the selfishness of their position, and do not remain untouched by the comradeship of women for women. As to prostitutes, I do not know how many or how few there are in our ranks. Neither does the Editor. But while I should consider it an impertinence to inquire, I should naturally not expect to find many, for the simple reason that their life, being anti-social by its very nature, they would be unlikely to join in a campaign of social reform. The aim of Suffragists is to cut off the supply of prostitutes by making other trades as profitable as that of prostitution, and by raising the status of women in the eyes of the public by removing the stigma of political sex inferiority branded on women by their votelessness. We are out against cheap women in any shape or form. That is a programme sufficiently wide and human to supply a complete transformation of current social values, whence, of course, the wall of opposition we are meeting.

With regard to Mr. Upton Sinclair, he has apparently not made himself acquainted with either the present position of English Suffragism or its history. The Common Cause, the organ of the oldest and largest suffrage society, is far more given to discussion of suffrage methods than the organ of the W.S.P.U. Moreover, the National Union has started a fighting policy which puts it in touch with Labour.

" July 7th, 1912."

We said: "The women's suffrage movement in England will doubtless be written of as the 'Idealess' movement. There are ideas in England, but there is no Idea behind English Suffragism. The Suffragists would like the vote, and they would like it now. Why? No reason, except that men have it. Suffragists have no reason except the one given above. They make up a few to suit their particular audiences as they go along. In their official capacity Suffragists are devoid of all social, political, or religious philosophy. . . . There is no feminism in Suffragism, nor is there any penetrating humanism. This explains why they have put forward no programme of demands. They have nothing to put forward specifically as their own. They think women are badly paid, and they think that prostitution is wrong. But they think these things from the outside and not from the inside." There was a sort of flirting interest taken in the subject of prostitution, but that this was unconsciously insincere, because officially it refused to consider either the psychology or the economics of the prostitution problem. "All things considered, therefore, Suffragists are safer without a programme."

This was the gist of our remarks, and we take it that Miss Willcocks does not question it. Rather, she prefers to meet the whole argument by a counter-argument, that not only is this so, but that it *should* be so, " since Suffragists are reformers of all schools of thought, whose common meeting-ground is that they believe in the political equality of men and women." There is an assumption in this kind of argument to which all suffrage societies hold, but which is plainly becoming untenable. It is the assumption that Suffragism can best be effected by concentration on Suffragism neat, as it were; that it is desirable to attack the problem by hitting it on the bulge. This is a theory of campaigning which, while being possible with small readjustments, is impossible with radical changes, tantamount, in the eyes of many, to a social revolution. Such radical changes can only find adequate defence as part of a tendency. The change in itself is merely an incident, and can be recognised as such, but when its adoption leads to the obliteration of features hitherto established, and to the creation of new and unconsidered features, then those who are timid about making the change have a right to ask what the idea is which is behind the change. The idea is the conception of the fact made fluid. It is delineation of its tendency. The idea makes plain where it is going. Conscious realisation of the tendency of a readjustment is what is meant by the possession of a philosophy regarding it.

Suffrage organisation, inasmuch as it wished to be vital, should have solidified according to belief, that is, according to tendency, to idea. But the suffrage "leaders" have been afraid to do this, because they feared to lose the conventional sympathies of those who naturally—honestly, we might even say—should have remained outside the movement altogether. We now begin to see the effects of this timidity. The organisations are permeated with the fear of expression of ideas in their ranks. Mental bullying is carried on inside their ranks to a remarkable extent. The "Idealess" hold the whip-hand over those who have ideas. The process goes quite long lengths in untruthfulness

and purposeful misstatement. We give a case in point. During the last three weeks, in the columns of the *Times*, a controversy initiated by Mrs. Humphry Ward has been carried on between herself and certain Suffragists. Mrs. Ward was very naturally, psychologically speaking, pointing out to Suffragists that the granting of the suffrage was bound up with a tendency which was leading to disintegrating changes which were untried and fraught with moral danger. Instancing the moral depths to which they might in time come, she gave ideas purporting to have been found in THE FREE-WOMAN. "Free" love, of course, was there, and Irreligion. The suffrage society which replied officially, through the person of a Miss Maude Royden, was the largest English society, i.e., the National Union of Woman Suffrage Societies. This letter contained the following:—

" If Mrs. H. Ward wishes to judge the suffrage movement fairly, she should surely read the literature and newspapers of the suffrage societies, and not an obscure little periodical which is neither published, owned, nor read by their members. She has, indeed, very much less right to hold us responsible for this nauseous publication than we have to judge her by Sir Almroth Wright's letter to you. But we accept her repudiation of his views, though they were circulated by her society, and we have a right to ask that she should accept ours.
" The literature of the N.U.W.SS. is, I believe, the fullest and most representative of any published by the larger suffrage associations. Let those who oppose us read it and oppose us for what we hold, not for what others hold, for whom we have no responsibility, and with whom we have no common ground. It is not good fighting, and it is not really effective, to set up a man of straw and knock it down; nor will Mrs. Humphry Ward find it easy to persuade the public that the Bishop of Oxford is really ' ranged ' with ' the ape and the tiger of the flesh.'

" A. MAUDE ROYDEN,
" Chairman of Literature Committee of N.U.W.S.S.
" N.U.W.S.S., Parliament Chambers, 14, Great Smith Street, Westminster, June 21st."

Now this representative of the National Union either knew of what she wrote or she did not. If she did not know (and it is difficult to understand how she could fail to know, or presume to write in the name of a bona-fide organisation did she not), she made the kind of deliberate misstatement which is commonly called lying. It is to be noted that no repudiation of her remarks has been forthcoming either from the National Union, from any other suffrage society, or from individual suffragists.

Yet the facts are that THE FREEWOMAN is read by some suffragists in every large suffrage society in England, in almost every country in Europe, all the colonies, and in India; while in America what is, we believe, the largest American suffrage society, at the request of its literature secretary, and endorsed by other committee members, is publishing certain of the articles which have appeared as leading articles in THE FREEWOMAN, in pamphlet form. This has been done spontaneously, at the Suffragists' cost, with profits accruing to THE FREEWOMAN. Concerning the members of the National Union in particular, the paper is subscribed to by " rank and file " members; by officials in London and throughout the provinces; officers and speakers of the Union have contributed articles to THE FREEWOMAN'S pages, one such being in the paper at the time of the controversy, and another, which was already accepted at that time, appearing in this issue. Some assistance to the circulation has been given by asking for requests for copies of the paper to be sent for sale or distribution at local meetings. Miss Willcocks herself is, we believe, a member of the same society, and is a reader and contributor to the paper.

Upon attention being drawn by Mrs. Humphry Ward to the fact that two certainly not unfavourable notices of THE FREEWOMAN had appeared in the editorial notices of the *Common Cause*, the organ of the National Society, the young person replied as follows:—

"In reply to Mrs. Humphry Ward's letter, I wish to point out that the first notice quoted by her from the *Common Cause* appeared when the paper referred to had only just been published, and already conveyed a criticism; the second (and last) was written only four weeks later, before the appearance of an article, which, to my mind, clearly showed the line that the new paper would take. Since then there has been no notice; and I confess that, had I been the editor of the *Common Cause*, I should have felt that silence was a better course than the gratuitous advertisement of denunciation. In this I feel sure Mrs. Ward will agree with me. . . .—Yours obediently,

"H. MAUDE ROYDEN,

"N.U.W.S.S., Parliament Chambers, 14, Great Smith Street, Westminster, S.W."

This is very subtle. It really means nothing, but the impression which it is calculated to convey is that after the appearance of a certain article, unnamed, the editorial attitude of the *Common Cause* changed so completely that even an adverse criticism might be reckoned a thing too good. From personal inference, we feel justified in saying that this implied meaning is as regardless of truth as were the earlier statements which it was intended to explain away.

Such things as these are not calculated to make us optimistic concerning the potentialities which inhere in organisations for "suffrage-neat." We all know of the hide-boundness of the Social and Political Union, and it probably strikes English people as strange that observant visitors like Mr. Upton Sinclair should have looked upon that society as the likeliest to adopt a forward and thought-inspired policy; but when we learn that even out of a democratically governed body like the Freedom League, seven of its foremost officials and workers have felt themselves compelled to retire, on the specific account of autocratic and arbitrary management; when we find that in the National Union, an official is permitted to use the entire prestige of the Union, to misrepresent the attitude of some of its most valued workers, and in order to injure, if possible, the sole medium for the interchange of ideas, be they right or wrong, which exists in the woman's movement, we become very reflective concerning the power of any organisation to remain healthy which restricts its inquiries to suffrage mainly. Suffrage propaganda, reaping its harvest of question for adequate *reasons*, necessitates advance forwards, backwards, or round in a circle. It is impossible to remain stationary. The W.S.P.U. have solved the problem cheaply by creating a fictitious movement. Militancy takes the place of thought-movement. *Their* problem, then, is solved for the time being. Militancy is the astutest possible move to keep thought quiet. But with the Freedom League and the National Union they have to find *momentum* in the thought, the philosophy, the tendency, which suffrage represents. Yet these Suffragists burk the preliminary collecting and weighing of evidence, the questioning as to where the movement

is going. Mrs. Humphry Ward or any Anti-Suffragist is speaking very pertinently when she points out there are vast possibilities as to what may follow in the wake of suffrage, and Suffragists, instead of accepting such criticism as a challenge, retort weakly with platitude and irrelevant and untruthful abuse. Yet, notwithstanding, the *tendency forces* them into movement—a movement dangerous in proportion to its uninformedness. The White Slave Traffic Bill is an instance to hand, a tinkering business, with advantages almost infinitesimal, and with very distinct and threatening disadvantages. We realise that the situation is big with danger when persons consider "nauseous" the open discussion of facts upon which they are prepared to rush into legislation which interferes with the liberty of their fellowmen and women upon suspicion.

The activities of our times make it clear that women are not remaining motionless because they have not as yet thought out any social or political philosophy. Nor do events stand still. Both move, and thought must move with them, if change is to be a blessing and not a curse.

Miss Willcocks says we hold Suffragists contemptible because they have not refused to live on rent-profit or interest, and have not repudiated marriage. This is not so. It is Miss Willcocks' own interpretation. We should say merely that such persons are acquiescing, perhaps unconsciously, in social injustice. It is when such persons strike the pose of ladies bountiful, that a little reflection becomes urgent. When cant sets in, it is time to speak out. To read the hectic oratory concerning prostitutes in a gathering called to consider the "Religious Aspects of the Woman's Movement" opens up a penetrating line of estimation as to the best method of dealing with all such phenomena. A douche of cold criticism will do no harm. Incipient hypocrisy can be browbeaten, and we will hope in this case we may have caught it young. For since *tendency* is acting, *as it must*, and since the Suffragists are beginning to experiment with the prostitute problem, they will do well to rid themselves of cant in the first instance, and, in a second, to reflect that this cancerous growth of prostitution has infected every civilisation since the beginning of human history, and that, therefore, some little knowledge of human character as it *is*, and not as they choose to imagine it, will be useful to them. Suffragists being in the nature of things driven into action, are tampering with the solution of problems, but when pertinent criticism is made regarding their method of approaching these, they say, "But we have no programme. We are getting the Vote." In our view, the whole assumption that suffragism can be approached without philosophy is false, and events are confirming our view, but we hold there is less danger in such an attitude, than in that which, while declaring there exists no programme officially, unofficially supports, with the whole weight of its organisation, schemes of legislation on intricate human problems, which have received nothing more than sentimental attention. Unless Suffragists mean to get understanding of these problems, it is altogether healthier, indeed, more honest, for them to stick to their straightforward, if mistaken, attitude of "No programme." Hence we finish our remarks with the phrase which closed our previous article on suffragism. "All things considered, Suffragists are safer without a programme. To want a vote, and want it now, is a small affair, but it has the merit of sincerity."

Bibliography

Note

This bibliography is organised into two categories – primary and secondary sources. The former is subdivided into two sections. The first refers to individual organisations in the following order: the NUWSS, the WFL, the WSPU, *The Freewoman*, Sylvia Pankhurst and lastly the 'antis'. The literature for each is arranged alphabetically by author or by date where no author is given. The second section refers to material relating to feminism and the women's suffrage movement published up to and including 1919. This is listed alphabetically by author.

The secondary sources category, which concentrates on feminism, women's history and the suffrage movement, is again listed alphabetically by author and refers to work published after 1919. In both categories and in all sections material not specifically alluded to in the text but of relevance to the feminism of the women's suffrage movement has been included too.

Primary Sources

The most important collections of suffragist and suffragette material are to be found at the Fawcett Library (now housed at the City of London Polytechnic) and at the London Museum. Others include the Maude Arncliffe-Sennet collection (British Library) and the archives held at the Manchester Central Reference Library. The British Newspaper Library, at Colindale, has complete collections of all newspapers referred to in the text.

Individual organisations
1. NUWSS. All at Fawcett Library.
   a. Annual Reports 1905–1919
   b. Newspapers: *The Women's Franchise* 1907–9; *Common Cause* 1909–18
   c. Pamphlets. Author given, published in London.
Chance, Lady (1913), *Women's Suffrage and Morality*
Creighton, Mrs (1913), *Women's Suffrage*
Fawcett, M.G. (c.1905), *Home and Politics*
   – (1912), *Broken Windows and After*
   – (1913), *Votes For Women: A Reply to Lloyd George*
   – (1916), *The New Parliamentary Register and Votes for Women*
   – (1917), *Speaker's Conference on Electoral Reform*
   – (1918), *The New Women Voters*
   – (1918), *Women and Their Use of the Vote*
   – (1927), *What the Vote Has Done*
Hodgson, C. (c.1909), *Five Points in the Relation Between Votes For Women and Certain Economic and Social Facts*
McLaren, Lady L. (1908), *Better and Happier*
Osler, Mrs A.C. (c.1911), *Why Women Need The Vote*

Royden, A. Maude (1909), *Physical Force and Democracy*
—(1911), *Votes and Wages: How Women's Suffrage Will Improve the Economic Position of Women*
– (1913), *The True End of Government*
– (1914), *Our Common Humanity*
Shillington, V.M. (c.1909), *Women Wage Earners and the Vote*
No author, arranged by date:
(1909), *Debate between Mrs Humphrey Ward and Mrs M. Fawcett 26th February 1909*
(1909), *Physical Force*
(1911), *Why Midwives and Nurses Need Votes*
(1912), *Anti-Suffragist Arguments*
(1912), *Let The Women Help*
(1912), *The Question of the Moment: The Real Issue of Women's Suffrage*
(1912), *Women In The Home*
(1912), *Women's Suffrage and the Protection of Women Workers. Will the Vote Help To Improve The Conditions of Their Work?*
(1913), *Parliament and The Children*
(1913), *Why Homekeeping Women Want The Vote*
(1914), *Election Fighting Fund*
(1914), *Votes for Mothers*
(1914), *Votes for Working Women*
(1916), *A Memorandum Showing Why Women Should Take Part in the Election of the Parliament Which is to Deal with Problems of Reconstruction Arising out of the War*
(1917), *Women and The Nation*
(1917), *Women Workers*
(1926), *Votes For the Women Left Out*
(1927), *Equal Franchise 1918–1928*
(1928), *A Manifesto To The New Voter – Why Should You Vote?*

2. WFL. In the London Museum unless otherwise stated.
   a. Minutes and Reports (Fawcett Library)
   b. Newspapers: *The Women's Franchise* 1907–9; *The Vote* (Fawcett Library)
   c. Pamphlets
Billington-Grieg, T. (1908), *Towards Women's Liberty*
– (1909), *Suffragist Tactics Past and Present*
– and Fitzherbert, M. (eds) (1909), *The Hour and the Woman*, Nos. 1–3
Boyle, C. Nina, (c.1913), *The Traffic in Women*
Campbell, Rev. R.J. (1908), *Women's Suffrage and the Social Evil*
– (1909), *Some Economic Aspects of the Women's Suffrage Movement*
Despard, Charlotte (1908), *Economic Aspects of Women's Suffrage*
– (1910), *Women's Franchise and Industry*
– (c.1911), *Women in the Nation*
Fitzherbert, M. (1910), *Lords v. Commons*
Holmes, M. (1910), *The ABC of Votes for Women*
Houseman, L. (1912), *Sex War and Women's Suffrage*
– (1914), *Be Law Abiding*
Murray, E.G. (1914), *The Illogical Sex*
Neilans, A. (1910), *Ballot Box Protest*

No author, arranged by date:
(1908) *Some Social Problems and Votes for Women* (Fawcett Library)
(1908), *Verbatim Report of Debate on December 3 1907: Sex Equality v. Adult Suffrage*
(1908), *The Women's Freedom League*
(1910), *What We Want to Do with the Vote*
(1910), *Why Women Want The Vote*

3. WSPU (and Women's Party). In the London Museum unless otherwise stated.
   a. Minutes and Reports (London Museum and Fawcett Library)
   b. Newspapers
      Votes for Women 1907–1912
      Suffragette 1912–1915 (Fawcett Library)
      Britannia 1915–1918 (British Library)
   c. Pamphlets
Gawthorpe, M. (c.1908), *Votes for Men: How They Were Won*
Houseman, L. (c.1908), *The Physical Force Fallacy*
John, N.A. (ed.) (1912), *Holloway Jingles*
Pankhurst, C. (1908), *The Militant Methods of the NWSPU*
  – (c.1911), *Some Questions Answered*
  – (1913), *The Great Scourge and How to End It*
  – (1914), *America and The War*
  – (1918), *Industrial Salvation*
Pankhurst, E. (1913), *Why We Are Militant*
  – (1914), *The Importance of the Vote*
Pethick-Lawrence, E. (c.1908a), *The Tactics of the Suffragettes*
  – (c.1908b), *The Meaning of the Women's Suffrage Movement*
  – (1911a), *A Call to Women*
  – (1911b), *Does a Man Support His Wife?*
  – (1913), *In Women's Shoes*
Pethick-Lawrence, F.W. (c.1908), *The Bye-Election Policy of the WSPU*
  – (c.1911), *Votes and Wages*
  – (1912), *The Man's Share*
Smith, Lady Sybil (c.1912), *Ethics of the Militant Movement*
Zangwill, I. (1910), *The Sword and the Spirit*
  No author, arranged by date:
(c.1906), *The ABC of Militant Methods*
(1907), NWSPU Circular (Maude Arncliffe-Sennet Collection)
(1912), *A Challenge*
(c.1912), *Our Demand: What It Is and What It Is Not*
(c.1912), *Why Women Want The Vote*
(1913), *The Outragettes*
(1917), *Women's Party Programme*

4. *The Freewoman*
   a. Marsden papers. Held by her niece, Mrs Bate.
   b. Newspapers (British Museum)
      The Freewoman 1911–1912
      The New Freewoman 1913–1914

5. The organisations of Sylvia Pankhurst. At the Institute of Social History, Amsterdam, unless otherwise stated.
1912–14: The East London Federation of the WSPU (ELFWSPU)
1914–16: The East London Federation of Suffragettes (ELFS)
1916–18: The Workers' Suffrage Federation (WSF)
1918–24: The Workers' Socialist Federation (WSF)
a. Minutes and Reports
b. Newspapers (British Museum)
   The Women's Dreadnought 1913–1917
   The Workers' Dreadnought 1917–1924
c. Pamphlets
Kollantai, A.M. (1920), *Communism and The Family*
Pankhurst, Sylvia (1913a), *To Every Woman*
 – (1913b), *Votes for Women*
 – (c.1914a), *Join the People's Army*
 – (1914b), *The Hunger and Thirst Strike and Its Effects*
 – (c.1917), *Workers! Demand Food and Peace*
 – (c.1918), *Education of the Masses*
 No authors, arranged by date:
(c.1913), *No Vote! No Rent!*
(1914), *Rent Strike and Food Supply*
(1915), *Down With Sweating*
(1915), *The Mothers' Arms*
(1915), *Votes for Women*
(1917), *The Workers' Suffrage Federation*
(1918), *How to Solve The Housing Question*

6. Women's National League for Opposing Women's Suffrage (WNLOWS) (later National League for Opposing Women's Suffrage)
a. Pamphlets
Barlow, G. (c.1910), *Why I Oppose Women's Suffrage*
Compton-Pickett, Sir J. (1912), *A Memorandum on Women's Suffrage*
Latham, F. (1910), *Thirty Reasons Why the Enfranchisement of Women Is Undesirable*
Page, A. (1912), *Women's Suffrage. Its Meaning and Effect*
 No author, arranged by date:
(14 August 1908), *Queen Victoria and Women's Rights* ('do not let us be afraid of being called stupid. We are stupid in good company; we stand side by side with Queen Victoria')
(28 August 1908), *Nature's Reason Against Suffrage*
(2 October 1908), *Why The Women's Enfranchisement Bill 1908 Would Be Unfair to Women If It Became Law*
(23 October 1908), *Women's Position Under Laws Made by Man*
(10 November 1908), *The Franchise for Women of Property*
(29 January 1909), *Women's Suffrage and After*
(29 January 1909), *Women's Suffrage and Women's Wages*
(18 February 1909), *Why Women Should Not Vote*
(18 February 1909), *Women's Suffrage and National Welfare*
(nd–c.1908), *Votes for Women*
(nd–c.1909), *A Word to Working Women*

Miscellaneous material relating to feminism and the women's suffrage movement up to 1918

A.J.R. (ed.) (1913), *The Suffrage Annual and Women's Who's Who*, London: Stanley Paul and Co.

Allan, G. (1906), *The Woman Who Did*, London: Grant Richards

Ashton, M., (1915), *Printed Circular from Margaret Ashton on Her Resignation*, Manchester

Bax, E.B. (1913), *The Fraud of Feminism*, London: Grant Richards

Bebel, F.A. (trans. Leon, D.D.) (1917), *Women and Socialism*, New York: Labour News Co.

Benson, T.D. (1906), *Woman The Communist*, London: ILP

Billington-Grieg, T. (c.1911), *The Militant Suffrage Movement – Emancipation in a Hurry*, London: F. Palmer

Black, C. (1906), *Sweated Industry and the Minimum Wage*, London: Duckworth and Co.

Blackburn, H. (1902), *Women's Suffrage – A Record of the Women's Suffrage Movement in The British Isles*, London: Williams and Norgate

Blease, G.W.L. (1910), *The Emancipation of English Women*, London: Constable

Brailsford, H.N., and Murray, J. (1911), *The Treatment of the Women's Deputations by the Metropolitan Police*, London

Carpenter, E. (1896), *Sex Love and Its Place in a Free Society*, Manchester: Labour Press

– (1896), *Loves Coming of Age. A Series of Papers on The Relations of the Sexes*, Manchester: Labour Press

Carter, H. (ed.) (1911), *Women's Suffrage and Militancy*, London: F. Palmer

Chesser, E.M.S. (1913), *Woman, Marriage and Motherhood*, London: Cassell

Cobbe, F.P. (1881), *Duties of Women*, London: Williams and Norgate

Davies, M. Llewellyn (1915), *Maternity – Letters From Working Women*, London: Bell

Fawcett, M.G. (1912), *Women's Suffrage – A Short History of a Great Movement*, London: T.C. and E.C. Jack

Ford, I.O. (1904), *Women and Socialism*, London: ILP

Gilman, C.P. (1906), *Women and Economics. A Study of the Economic Relation Between Men and Women As a Factor in Social Evolution*, London: Putnam

Goldman, E. (1910), *Anarchism and Other Essays*, New York: Mother Earth

Grayson, V., Taylor, G.R.S. (1909), *The Problem of Parliament – A Criticism and A Remedy*, London: New Age Press

Hamilton, C. (1909), *Marriage As A Trade*, London: Chapman and Hall

Hardie, J.K. (1907), *From Serfdom to Socialism*, London: G. Allen

– (1906), *The Citizenship of Women* (pamphlet), London: ILP

Jenks, E. (1909), *Husband and Wife In Law*, London, Dent

Jones, L.M. (1914), *Report on Miss Gordon, Suffragist Prisoner in Perth* (Maude Arncliffe-Sennet Collection)

Key, E.S. (1912), *The Woman Movement*, London: Putnam

London, J. (1903), *The People of the Abyss*, London: Isbister

Lytton, Lady Constance (1909), *'No Votes For Women', a reply to some recent anti-suffrage publications*, London: Fifield

McLaren, Lady L. (1910), *The Women's Charter of Rights and Liberties*, London: Grant Richards

Martindale, L. (1910), *Under the Surface*, Brighton

Metcalfe, A.E. (1917), *Woman's Effort 1865–1914: A Chronicle of British Women's Fifty Years Struggle For Citizenship*, Oxford: Blackwell

– (1919), *'At Last' Conclusion of 'Woman's Effort'*, Oxford: Blackwell

Mill, J.S. (1869), *On The Subjection of Women*, 2nd edn, London: Longmans, Green, Reader and Dyer

Pankhurst, S. (1911), *The Suffragette – The History of the Women's Militant Suffrage Movement 1905–1910*, New York: Sturgis and Walton

Roberts, K. (1911), *Pages from the Diary of a Militant Suffragette*, London: Garden City Press

Schreiner, O. (1911), *Women and Labour*, London: Fisher Unwin

Snowden, E. (1907), *The Woman Socialist*, London: Grant Allen

– (1913), *The Feminist Movement*, London: Collins

'Sophia' (1739), *Woman Not Inferior to Man* (or a short and modest vindication of the natural right of the fair sex to a perfect equality of power, dignity and esteem, with the men), London: Hawkins

Swanwick, H.M.L. (1913), *Future of the Women's Movement*, London: Bell

– (1914), *Some Points of English Law Affecting Working Women As Wives and Workers*, London: Women's Co-operative Guild (WCG)

Thompson, W. (1825), *Appeal of One Half of the Human Race, Women, Against the Pretensions of the Other Half, Men, to Retain Them in Political and Thence Civil and Domestic Slavery*, London: Longmans.

Wilkinson, L.G. (c.1910), *Revolutionary Socialism and the Woman's Movement*, Glasgow: Socialist Labour Party

– (1914), *Women's Freedom*, London: Freedom Press

Wollstonecraft, M. (1787), *Thoughts on the Education of Daughters*, London

– (1792), *A Vindication of the Rights of Women: With Strictures on Political and Moral Subjects*, London: J. Johnson

Women's Co-operative Guild (1911), *Working Women and Divorce. An Account of Evidence Given on Behalf of the WCG Before the Royal Commission on Divorce*, London: WCG

Wright, Sir Almroth, E. (1913), *The Unexpurgated Case Against Women's Suffrage*, London: Constable

Secondary Sources

Adam, R. (1975), *A Woman's Place 1910–1975*, London: Chatto and Windus

Adelmann, P. (1972), *The Rise of the Labour Party 1880–1945*, London: Longman

Aldred, G. (1956), *No Traitors Gait*, Glasgow: Strickland Press.

Ashdown-Sharp (1977), 'Women's Rights: The Missed Opportunity', *Sunday Times*, February 20, pp 17–18

Banks, J.A., and O. (1964), *Feminism and Family Planning in Victorian England*, Liverpool: Liverpool University

Berg, B.J. (1978), *The Remembered Gate: Origins of American Feminism*, Oxford: Oxford University Press

Blake, R. (1972), *The Conservative Party From Peel to Churchill*, London: Fontana

Blewitt, N. (1972), *The Peers, The Parties and The People: The General Election of 1910*, London: Macmillan

Brittain, V. (1960), *A Testament of Youth*, London: Arrow Books

C.I.S. Counter Information Services (1976), *Crisis: Women Under Attack*, London: CIS

Close, D.H. (1977), 'The Collapse of Resistance to Democracy: Conservatives, Adult Suffrage and 2nd Chamber Reform 1911–1928', *Historical Journal* Vol.20, No.4

Cole, G.D.H. and Postgate, R.S. (1938), *The Common People 1746–1938*, London: Methuen

Comer, L. (1971), *The Myth of Motherhood*, London: Spokesman

Conservative Central Office (1980), *Women In Politics*, London: CCO

Coote, A., and Campbell, B. (1982), *Sweet Freedom – The Struggle For Women's Liberation*, London: Picador

Dangerfield, G. (ed.) (1970), *Strange Death of Liberal England*, London: Paladin

Davin, A. (1978), 'Imperialism and Motherhood in History', *History Workshop Journal*, V, Spring 1978, Oxford: History Workshop

Delamont, S., Duffin, L. (1978), *The Nineteenth Century Woman: Her Cultural and Physical World*, London: Croom Helm

Dewar, H. (1976), *Communist Politics in Britain: The CPGB From Its Origins to the Second World War*, London: Pluto

Doughan, D. (1980), *Lobbying for Liberation: British Feminism 1918–1968*, London: City of London Polytechnic

Drake, B. (1920), *Women in Trades Unions*, London: Labour Research

Eisenstein, Z.R. (ed.) (1979), *Capitalist Patriarchy and the Case for Socialist Feminism*, New York: Monthly Review Press

Emy, H.V. (1973), *Liberals, Radicals and Social Politics 1892–1914*, Cambridge: Cambridge University Press

Ensor, R.C.K. (1936), *England 1817 to 1914*, Oxford: Clarendon Press

Equal Opportunities Commission (1977), *Women and Low Incomes*, Manchester: EOC

Fawcett, M.G.F. (1920), *The Women's Victory and After: Personal Reminiscences 1911–1918*, London: Sidgwick and Jackson

– (1924), *What I Remember*, London: Fisher and Unwin

Federici, S. (1975), *Wages Against Housework*, Bristol: Falling Wall Press

Feminist Practice (1979), *Notes from the Tenth Year*, London: In Theory Press

Firestone, S. (1972), *The Dialectic of Sex: The Case for Feminist Revolution*, London: Paladin

Fryer, P. (1965), *The Birth Controllers*, London: Secker and Warburg

Fulford, R. (1957), *Votes for Women*, London: Faber and Faber

Gallacher, W. (1966), *The Last Memoirs of William Gallacher*, London: Lawrence and Wishart

Gawthorpe, M. (1962), *Up the Hill to Holloway*, Maine: Traversity Press

Glass, D.V., (1938), 'Marriage Frequency and Economic Fluctuations in England and Wales 1851–1934', in Hogben, L. (ed.), *Political Arithmetic – A Symposium of Population Studies*, London: Allen and Unwin

– (1967), *Population Policies and Movements*, London

Groves, R. (1975), *The Strange Case of Victor Grayson*, London: Pluto Press

Halevy, E. (1952), *A History of the English People in the Nineteenth Century*, 2nd edn, London: Benn. Vol. 5, *Imperialism and the Rise of Labour – 1895–1905*; Vol. 6, *The Rule of Democracy*

Hamilton, C. (1935), *Life Errant*, London: Dent

Hamilton, R. (1978), *The Liberation of Women: A Study of Patriarchy and Capitalism*, London: Allen and Unwin

Harrison, B. (1978a), *Separate Spheres: The Opposition to Women's Suffrage*, London: Croom Helm

– (1978b) 'The Antis Last Stand', *Guardian*, May 4 p.11

Hay, J.R. (1975), *The Origins of the Liberal Welfare Reforms – 1906–1914*, London: Macmillan

Hill, C. (1969), *Reformation to Industrial Revolution*, Harmondsworth: Penguin

Hill, C.P. (1977), *British Economic and Social History*, London: Edward Arnold

Hinton, J. (1973), *The First Shop Stewards Movement*, London: Allen and Unwin

Hobsbawm, E.J. (1969), *Industry and Empire*, Harmondsworth: Pelican

Holtby, W. (1934), *Women and a Changing Civilisation*, London: John Lane

Hussey, W.D. (1971), *British History 1815–1939*, London: Cambridge University Press

Kamm, J. (1965), *Hope Deferred. Girls Education in English History*, Metheun

– (1966), *Rapiers and Battleaxes. The Women's Movement and its Aftermath*, London: Allen and Unwin

Kendall, W. (1969), *The Revolutionary Movement in Britain 1900–1921: The Origins of British Communism*, London: Weidenfeld and Nicolson

Kenney, A. (1924), *Memories of a Militant*, London: Edward Arnold

Klein, V. (1971), *The Feminine Character: History of an Ideology*, London: Routledge and Kegan Paul

Koss, S. (1976), *Asquith*, London: Allen Lane

Kraditor, A. (1965), *The Ideas of the Women's Suffrage Movement 1890–1920*, New York: Columbia University Press

Lewenhak, S. (1977), *Women and Trade Unions. An Outline of Women in the British Trade Union Movement*, London: Benn

Lidderdale, J.H., and Nicholson, M. (1970), *Dear Miss Weaver: Harriet Shaw Weaver 1876–1961*, London: Faber and Faber

Liddington, J., Norris, J. (1978), *One Hand Tied Behind Us: The Rise of the Women's Suffrage Movement*, London: Virago

Linklater (1980), *An Unhusbanded Life –Charlotte Despard: Suffragette, Socialist and Sinn Feiner*, London: Hutchinson

Lowry, S. (1980a), 'Housewives: Women Possessed?', *Observer*, April 20, p. 45

– (1980b), 'The Big Chap Out', *Observer*, August 3, p.34

McGregor, O.R. (1955), 'The Social Position of Women in England 1850–1914, A Bibliography', *British Journal of Sociology*, Vol. 6, No. 1., March

Malinowski, B. (1967), *Sex, Culture and Myth*, London: Mayflower

Marcus, S. (1969), *The Other Victorians: A Study of Sexuality and Pornography in Mid-Nineteenth Century England*, London: Corgi

Martyn, E. and Breed, M. (1930), *The Birth Control Movement in England*, London: J. Bale and Co.

Matthew, H.C.G. (1973), *The Liberal Imperialists: The Ideas and Politics of a Post-Gladstonian Elite*, Oxford: Oxford University Press

Mead, M. (1935), 'Sex and Temperament in Three Primitive Societies', in Schur, E.M. (ed. 1966), *The Family and the Sexual Revolution*, London: Allen and Unwin

Mitchell, B.R., Deane, P. (1962), *Abstract of British Historical Statistics*, Cambridge: Cambridge University Press

Mitchell, D. (1966), *Women on the Warpath*, London: Cape
– (1967), *The Fighting Pankhursts: A Study in Tenacity*, London: Cape
– (1970), 'Ghost of a Chance: British Revolutionaries in 1919', *History Today*, Vol. 20, November
– (1977), *Queen Christabel. A Biography of Christabel Pankhurst*, London: MacDonald and Jane
– (1978), How They Won The Vote, *Guardian*, May 3, p.11
Mitchell, J. (1971), *Women's Estate*, Harmondsworth: Penguin
Mitchell, J. and Oakley, A. (eds) (1976), *The Rights and Wrongs of Women*, Harmondsworth: Penguin
Mitchell, H. (1968), *The Hard Way Up: Autobiography of Hannah Mitchell, Suffragette and Rebel*, London: Faber and Faber
Montefiore, D.E. (1927), *From A Victorian to A Modern*, London: Archer
Morgan, D. (1975), *Suffragists and Liberals: The Politics of Women's Suffrage in Britain*, Oxford: Blackwell
Myrdal, A. and Klein, V. (1968), *Women's Two Roles*, Home and Work, London: Routledge and Kegan Paul
Neale, R.S. (1972), *Class and Ideology in the Nineteenth Century*, London: Routledge and Kegan Paul
Newbury, J.V. (1977), 'Anti-War Suffragists', *History – The Journal of the Historical Association*, Vol. 62, No. 206
Newsome, S. (c.1957), *The Women's Freedom League 1907–1957*, London: Women's Freedom League
Nield Chew, D. (1982), *The Life and Writings of Ada Nield Chew*, Virago
Oakley, A. (with J. Mitchell) (1972), *Sex, Gender and Society*, London: Temple Smith
Oakley, A. (1979), 'The Failure of The Movement for Women's Equality in New Society', *New Statesman*, Vol. 49, No. 881, August 23
Pankhurst, C. (1929), *Seeing The Future*, London: Harper
– (1959), *Unshackled: Or How We Won The Vote*, Hutchinson
Pankhurst, S. (1921), *Soviet Russia As I Saw It*, London: Dreadnought
– (1931), *The Suffragette Movement: An Intimate Account of Persons and Ideals*, London: Longman
– (1932), *The Home Front: A Mirror to Life in England During The World War*, London: Hutchinson
Pankhurst, R.K.P. (1954), *William Thompson, (1775–1833) – Britain's Pioneer Socialist, Feminist and Co-operator*, London: Longman
– (1979), *Sylvia Pankhurst. Artist and Crusader*, London: Paddington Press
Pearsall, R. (1971), *The Worm in The Bud: The World of Victorian Sexuality*, Harmondsworth: Penguin
Pelling, H. (1958), *The British Communist Party –A Historical Profile*, London: Black
Pelling, H. (with Bealey, F.) *Labour and Politics 1900–1906*
– (1958), *A History of the Labour Representation Committee*, London: Macmillan
– (1968), *Popular Politics and Society in Late Victorian Britain*, London: Macmillan
Pethick-Lawrence, E. (1938), *My Part in a Changing World*, London: Victor Gollanz
Pethick-Lawrence, F.W. (1943), *Fate Has Been Kind*, London: Hutchinson

Philips, P. (1980), 'When a Woman's Place is in the Commons', *The Guardian*, May 13, p. 8

Pinchbeck, I. (1930), *Women Workers and the Industrial Revolution 1750–1850*, London: Routledge

Pugh, M. (1977), 'Politicians and the Women's Vote 1914–1918', *Historical Journal*, Vol.20, no. 4

– (1978), *Electoral Reform in War and Peace 1906–1918*, London: Routledge and Kegan Paul

Raeburn, A. (1973), *The Militant Suffragettes*, London: Michael Joseph

Ramelson, M. (1967), *Petticoat Rebellion: A Century of Struggle for Women's Rights*, London: Lawrence and Wishart

Richards, E. (1974), 'Women in the British Economy Since About 1700: An Interpretation', *History – Journal of the Historical Association*, Vol. 59

Richardson, M.R. (1953), *Laugh a Defiance*, London: Weidenfeld and Nicolson

Rosen, D. (1974), *The Militant Campaign of the Women's Social and Political Union 1903–1914*, London: Routledge and Kegan Paul

Rover, C. (1967), *Women's Suffrage and Party Politics in Britain 1866–1914*, London: Routledge and Kegan Paul

– (1967), *Punch Book of Women's Rights*, London: Hutchinson

– (1970), *Love, Morals and the Feminists*, London: Routledge and Kegan Paul

Rowbotham, S. (1972), *Women's Liberation and Revolution A Bibliography*, Bristol: Falling Wall Press

– (1973), *Women's Consciousness, Man's World*, Harmondsworth: Penguin

– (1974), *Women, Resistance and Revolution*, Harmondsworth: Penguin

– (1977a), *Hidden From History: 300 Years of Women's Oppression and the Fight Against It*, London: Pluto Press

– (1977b), *A New World for Women: Stella Browne, Socialist and Feminist*, London: Pluto Press

Rowbotham, S., Segal, L., and Wainright, H. (1979), *Beyond the Fragments*, London: Merlin Press

Rowbotham, S. and Weeks, J. (1977), , *Socialism and the New Life: The Personal and Sexual Politics of Edward Carpenter and Havelock Ellis*, London: Pluto Press

Saywell, R.T. (1936), *Development of the Feminist Idea in England 1789–1853*, unpublished M.A. thesis, London University

Schneir, M. (ed.) (1972), *Feminism: The Essential Historical Writing*, New York: Vintage Books

Searle, G. (1971), *The Quest For National Efficency: A Study In British Politics and Political Thought 1899–1914*, Oxford: Blackwell

Secombe, W. (1974), 'The Housewife and Her Labour under Capitalism', *New Left Review*, No. 83

Semmel, B. (1960), *Imperialism and Social Reform: English Social Imperial Thought 1895–1914*, London: Macmillan

Sharpe, S. (1976), *Just Like a Girl. How Girls Learn to Be A Woman*, Harmondsworth: Penguin

Skinner, Q. (1969), 'Meaning and Understanding in the History of Ideas' in *History and Theory*, Vol. 8, No. 1

Strachey, R. (1928), *The Cause: A Short History of the Women's Movement in Great Britain*, London: Bell and Sons

– (1931), *Millicent Garrett Fawcett*, London: Murray

– (ed.) (1936), *Our Freedom and Its Results*, London: L.V. Woolf

Swanwick, H.M. (1935), *I Too Have Been Young*, London: Victor Gollancz

Taylor, A.J. (1964), *The Economy* in Nowell-Smith, S. *Edwardian England 1901–1914*, London: Oxford University Press

Thompson, P. (1975), *The Edwardians: The Remaking Of British Society*, London: Weidenfeld and Nicolson

Toynbee, P. (1978), 'What Happened to the Girls?', *The Guardian*, June 19

Wandor, M. (ed.) (1973), *The Body Politic – Women's Liberation in Britain 1969–1972*, London: Stage 1

Zaretsky, E. (1976), *Capitalism, The Family and Personal Life*, London: Pluto Press

Index

abortion
 growth in cases of in late C19th and early
 C20th, 6; reference to in NUWSS, 22
Abortion Law Reform Association, 67, 111
Actresses Franchise League, 5
adult suffrage
 problem for socialist suffragists, 4, 17; and
 ELFS calls for, 82; ELFS committed to, 86
Aldred, Guy
 contributor to *The Freewoman*, 62; criticism of
 WSPU militancy, 63, 105; on free love
 unions, 66; on the family, 72; on
 relationship between the sexes, 75; on
 syndicalism, 75
Allen, Grant, *The Woman Who Did*, 5
anarchism and suffragism, 4
Anderson, Elizabeth Garrett, 5
anti-suffragism
 and physical force argument, 7; party political
 motives behind, 7
Ashton, Margaret, resignation from NUWSS
 Executive Committee 1915, 24–5
Astor, Nancy, first woman MP to take her seat,
 109
Asquith, H.H.
 opposition to votes for women, 7; promise to
 allow suffrage amendment to 1913 Reform
 Bill, 16; on WSPU militancy, 49; reply to
 East End deputation June 1914, 81; 94;
 100; on failure of amendment to 1913
 Reform Bill, 98; influence of suffrage
 movement on, 98–100

Baldwin, Stanley 97
Balfour, Lady Frances 84
Beale, Dorothea 5
Besant, Annie 6
Besant–Bradlaugh trial 1877 6; 45
Bermondsey Ballot-Box 'outrage' 1909 29
Beveridge, Sir William, on women's roles after
 the Second World War 113
Billington-Greig, Teresa
 split from WSPU 28–9; association with ILP
 35; on Charlotte Despard 30; resignation
 from WFL 43; on WSPU electoral policy
 45; criticism of WSPU 59–60; *The Militant
 Suffrage Movement – Emancipation In A
 Hurry* 59–60; in *The Freewoman* 62;
 criticism of the Pankhursts 64; the limit of
 the vote 104; on militancy 105
Birnstingl, Harry J. 67
birth control
 available methods C19th, early C20th 6;
 discussion in NUWSS 21–2; in WFL
 39–40; in WSPU, *The Freewoman*, and

Sylvia Pankhursts organisations 90; and
 suffragism 106
Black, Clementina 7; 11; 12
'Black Friday' November 18 1910 48
Blake, Sophia Jex 5
Blatchford, Robert 4
Boord, Caroline *x*, 114
Booth, Charles 8
Bowlby, John 113
Boyle, Nina, on women's suffrage victory 103,
 109
Brailsford and Murray, *The Treatment of the
 Women's Deputation By The Metropolitan
 Police* (1911) 48
Bristol Fabian Women's Group 72
British Union of Fascists (BUF) 59
British Socialist Party (BSP)
 links with WFL 36–7; links with ELFS 85
Britannia
 replaces *The Suffragette* 55; temporary
 suspension during war 55
Browne, Edith 70
Browne, F.W. Stella 62
 on sexuality 67; criticism of Eugenicism 69;
 112
Burns, John 8
Butler, Josephine 6

Campbell, Rev. R.J., *Some Economic Aspects of
 the Women's Suffrage Movement* (1909) 32–3
Carpenter, Edward
 Loves Coming of Age (1896) 4; views on women
 4; and Millicent Garrett Fawcett 21; views
 reflected in *The Vote* 33; on *The Freewoman*
 62; on marriage 65
Carpenter, Mary 5
'Cat and Mouse' Act 1913 49
Chance, Lady 11
Chattle, Edith 20
Chew, Ada Nield *xi*, 12, 18
 articles in *Common Cause* 19–20; in *The
 Freewoman* 62; on *The Freewoman* 65; on
 economic independence and the maternal
 role 69–70; criticism of suffragist leaders
 75; on working class women and suffragism
 75; on *The Freewoman's* criticism of
 suffragism 120
Clough, Anne 5
Cobbe, Frances Power *Duties of Women* (1881) 4
Cohen, George 90
Common Cause, Organ of the NUWSS
 origins and development 12; editors 12
Communal Cafés
 NUWSS call for 14; and ELFS 83; and WSF
 92